HAWAIIAN HISTORICAL LEGENDS

BOOKS BY
WILLIAM D. WESTERVELT

Hawaiian Legends of Ghosts and Ghost Gods
Hawaiian Legends of Old Honolulu
Hawaiian Legends of Volcanoes

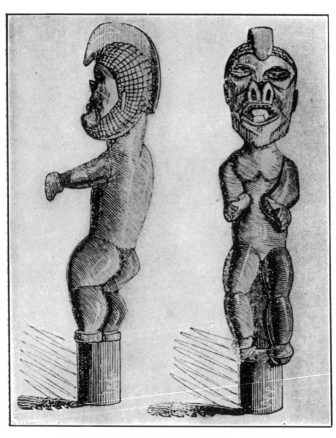

IDOLS BY WHICH CAPTAIN COOK WAS
WORSHIPPED

(*See page 108*)

HAWAIIAN HISTORICAL LEGENDS

by
William D. Westervelt

with an introduction to the new edition by
Terence Barrow, Ph.D.

Charles E. Tuttle Company
Rutland, Vermont & Tokyo, Japan

Representatives

Continental Europe: BOXERBOOKS, INC., *Zurich*

British Isles: PRENTICE-HALL INTERNATIONAL, INC., *London*

Australasia: BOOK WISE (AUSTRALIA) PTY. LTD.
104-108 Sussex Street, Sydney 2000

Published by the Charles E. Tuttle Company, Inc.
of Rutland, Vermont & Tokyo, Japan
with editorial offices at
Suido 1-chome, 2-6, Bunkyo-ku, Tokyo, Japan

Copyright in Japan, 1977, by Charles E. Tuttle Co., Inc.

Library of Congress Catalog Card No. 76-434060

International Standard Book No. 0-8048-1216-0

First edition, 1923
by Fleming H. Revell Co., New York
First Tuttle edition, 1977
Sixth printing, 1985

PRINTED IN JAPAN

CONTENTS

List of Illustrations 1
Introduction to the New Edition . . . 3
Preface 11

CHAPTER

I. Maui the Polynesian 13
II. Maui Seeking Immortality . . 19
III. The Water of Life 24
IV. A Viking of the Pacific . . . 35
V. Home of the Polynesians . . . 41
VI. Sons of Kii 47
VII. Paao from Samoa 65
VIII. Moikeha the Restless 79
IX. Laa from Tahiti 86
X. First Foreigners 93
XI. Captain Cook 100
XII. The Ivory of Oahu 114
XIII. The Alapa Regiment 125
XIV. The Last Prophet of Oahu . . 143
XV. The Eight of Oahu 149
XVI. The Red Mouth Gun 155
XVII. The Law of the Splintered Paddle 162
XVIII. Last of the Tabu 176
XIX. First Hawaiian Printing . . . 183
XX. The First Constitution . . . 189
XXI. The Hawaiian Flag 200
Index 217

ILLUSTRATIONS

FACING
PAGE

IDOLS BY WHICH CAPTAIN COOK WAS
   WORSHIPPED . . . . *Title page*

SPEAR THROWING CONTEST 62

CHIEFS IN FEATHER CLOAKS AND HELMETS . 88

LANDING OF WARRIORS 134

HAWAIIAN GRASS HOUSES 172

FIRST LEAFLET PRINTED, 1822 184

TITLE PAGE OF FIRST HYMN BOOK, 1823 . . 186

FIRST BIBLE PRINTING, 1827 188

INTRODUCTION TO THE
NEW EDITION

HAWAIIAN legends and historical stories written by Dr. W. D. Westervelt remain popular for good reason. They are stories well told. The original editions of his books have become rare collector's items. However, reprints of several Westervelt titles have put these charming books once more into the hands of the general public. These include: *Hawaiian Legends of Ghosts and Ghost Gods, Hawaiian Legends of Old Honolulu, Hawaiian Legends of Volcanoes,* and now *Hawaiian Historical Legends.*

Hawaiian Historical Legends presents a variety of stories, both legendary and historical. The author also considers the question of Polynesian origins and the speculative subject of Spanish visitants. Since anthropological and historical research has come half a century since this book was written, it would be appropriate in this introduction to provide the non-specialist reader with more up-to-date observations. For example, Dr. Westervelt rejects the suggestion that Samoa was an early Polynesian homeland, yet modern science says that Samoa along with Tonga—an area settled by proto-Polynesians about a thousand years before Christ—

served as a primary base where distinctive Polynesian culture first put down its roots. Polynesia, meaning "many islands," was never known to old-time Polynesians; it is the word Western scholars coined for that South Sea region and its people.

Who were the Polynesians? Who were the Hawaiians? Where did they come from? The answer is now clear, in outline at least. Malayo-Polynesian groups occupied vast areas of Indonesia and the coastal regions of Asia for several millennia. Some, in search of new homes, ventured out into the Pacific in their canoes, gradually finding and settling islands. The voyages they planned for the purpose included their children, women, dogs, pigs, fowls, and food plants. The story is a marvel of human endeavor and courage, particularly as their technology was not past the neolithic or polished stone-tool level of development.

Before European seafarers dared to leave the coastal waters of the eastern Atlantic, these sea gypsies of the Pacific had settled the far-flung islands of Polynesia.

The islands on the western fringes of Polynesia, namely Samoa and Tonga, are believed to have been first occupied about three thousand years ago. By the ninth century this remarkable people had discovered and settled all the habitable islands in the Polynesian triangle—an area encompassed by New Zealand to the south, Easter Island to the east, and Hawaii to the north.

Anthropologists say Hawaii was first settled about the eighth century from the Marquesas Islands. Later, in the fourteenth century, it seems that warlike immigrants from the Society Islands came to Hawaii's shores and imposed on the aboriginal settlers their religion, customs, and their own aristocracy.

Hawaiian culture, as it existed when Captain James Cook found the islands in 1778, was an amalgam of these two Polynesian peoples. As both groups shared many of the same gods, culture heroes, and specific stories, the mythological tradition merged without difficulty or conflict.

Much knowledge has been lost, but the labors of men such as Judge A. Fornander put much into written language (e.g., *An Account of the Polynesian Race*). Even though he worked in a comparatively late era, Dr. Westervelt makes a valuable contribution to the preservation of Hawaiian legends. In retelling these stories he relied to a large extent on his excellent library.

Many old-time Polynesians preferred to die with their learning rather than pass it on; they regarded such information as too sacred a trust. To them it was esoteric knowledge. The traditional way of preserving information, in the absence of any written script, was to cultivate the memory. Recitation by rhythmical chant was usual and absolute accuracy was expected of the trained person. Any error, such as an omitted word, could cause disaster. Misfortune and even death itself were thought to result from such carelessness. Maui, the semi-divine Polynesian superman about whom Dr. Westervelt writes, received a fatal flaw when his father made a mistake at Maui's baptismal ritual. For this reason Maui became vulnerable to death and, ironically, he died while seeking immortality for mankind.

The termination of the great tradition of rote learning as a means of preserving tribal history, genealogy, events, and sacred lore declined rapidly after the rejection by the Hawaiians of their religion in 1819—just before the arrival of the first New England missionary party. The introduction of pen, paper, and books made rigid memorizing obsolete, while the need for such a system had waned with the destruction of the old ways.

A written Hawaiian language literally began the day Captain James Cook romanized Hawaiian words in his journal and on his maps. However, the adoption of a set Hawaiian alphabet, and a general agreement as to how to spell Hawaiian words, were the later work of committees of New England missionaries who needed to translate books of the Bible and to teach writing.

In reading these stories we should keep in mind the nature of traditional Hawaiian culture and its ancient attitudes toward nature with its belief in *aumakua*—a spirit world of gods, ghosts, ancestral spirits, and totemic creatures (such as the owl, shark, and lizard). To the traditional Hawaiians all the things of nature such as the sea, sky, earth, animals, fish, rocks—and even such unsubstantial objects as the rainbow—were thought to have an indwelling spirit and a personal existence. There was no clear division in the Polynesian mind between man, the spirit world, and the natural environment. Interpretations of the world were poetic and not scientific.

All things were seen as having an inner essence, called *mana*, which was the vital force of an object. This mana was protected by taboos (*kapu* in Hawaiian), which were a collection of prohibitions that protected the part of a person or thing which gave power and effectiveness. Kapu was inconvenient, and dangerous if infringed. Many a slave or commoner died for letting his shadow fall across a seated chief—mana had been interfered with and a kapu broken! Such was the law of old Hawaii. No police force was necessary.

Once discovered by Captain James Cook for the Western world, the Hawaiian islands became a convenient refreshment place for exploring expeditions, whalers, sandalwood traders and the like. A half-century of such contacts passed before the arrival of the missionaries who introduced the semblance of Western society and social order. Before the arrival of the missionaries, various drifters, beachcombers, and adventurers, both good and bad, imposed themselves on the Hawaiians. Everybody who came wanted something of the Hawaiian people, whether

it was wood, water, pigs, potatoes, women, or sandalwood. It says much for Hawaiian patience that
more ships were not taken and more heads broken
by clubs.

Dr. Westervelt uses the old forms of Hawaiian
spelling. There are no hamzas to mark the glottal
closures or macrons to indicate a vowel lengthened
in pronunciation. But in the interest of preserving
this unusual collection intact, it was decided to let
the book stand exactly as it was first published.

It is, however, necessary to draw attention to the
two controversial issues raised by Dr. Westervelt
that have been since resolved. The first is the
question of a pre-Cook Spanish discovery of the
Hawaiian Islands, and the second is the charge that
Captain Cook was an immoral man and a dese-
crater of temples.

The truth is, no scholar has succeeded in establish-
ing any historical evidence for a Spanish discovery
prior to that of Captain Cook. As for the character
of Cook, he was a singularly chaste man who declined all offers of women. This unusual behavior
for a sailor was even remarked on by the men who
sailed with him and who best knew his habits. As for
the allegation that Cook desecrated a Hawaiian
temple, the structure concerned was in decay and
the wooden fences around it were taken by
Cook's men after the Hawaiians had given their
permission and received payment for the wood. The
Hawaiians probably intended that only the fence

be removed, but the sailors assigned to the job had little respect for images of gods and took them too. It was a shocking act to which Cook was not a part, and when the Hawaiians asked for the return of one particular figure it was given to them.

The story, "The Ivory of Oahu," also calls for some explanation. It would help the uninformed reader to know that a special type of necklace of old Hawaii was made from the tooth of a sperm whale carved into a hook-like form, then suspended with yards of finely plaited human hair looped many times and passed through a hole drilled in the tooth. This ornament is called a *lei-niho-palaoa,* which means a lei or necklace with a whale tooth. Such necklaces were worn only by persons of high rank. The hair used to make them was probably from the head of an important person, such as an immediate ancestor, and they were precious and kapu. (The head was the most sacred part of the body; the mere touching of a chief's head was a death warrant to a commoner.)

Dr. Westervelt came to Hawaii in 1889 for two years of missionary work. After a brief return to the United States mainland, he came back to the islands in 1905 where he lived until his death in 1939. He married a Miss Caroline D. Castle of a pioneer missionary family and settled down to an active life of preaching, writing, and helping others in his adopted society. The Westervelt home at Waikiki was for decades a democratic gathering place for those interested in art, music, or literature. Regardless of race, creed, or rank, all were welcome.

Dr. Westervelt did as much as anyone to popularize Hawaiian legends and historical tales. On the dedication page he refers to *Hawaiian Historical Legends* as his sixth book; it is certainly one of his most charming collections of stories. First published in 1923, this book went through several editions in the 1920s, but until now it has not been readily available for several decades.

Terence Barrow, Ph.D.

PREFACE

From mist to sunshine—from fabled gods to a constitution and legislature as a Territory of the United States—this is the outline of the stories told in the present volume. This outline is thoroughly Hawaiian in the method of presentation. The old people rehearsed stories depending upon stories told before. They cared very little for dates. This is a book of stories related to each other.

Veiled by the fogs of imagination are many interesting facts concerning kings and chiefs which have been passed over untouched—such as the voyages of the vikings of the Pacific, who left names and legends around the islands. For instance, Hilo, in the island of Hawaii, is named after Whiro, a noted viking who sailed through many island groups with his brother, Punga, after whom the district of Puna is named. Ka-kuhi-hewa, ruler of Oahu, was the King Arthur of the Hawaiians, with a band of noted chiefs around his poi-bowl. Umi was a remarkable king of the island Hawaii. Many individual incidents of these persons are yet to be related.

The Hawaiian language papers since 1835, Fornander's Polynesian Researches, and many of the old Hawaiians have been of great assistance in searching for these "fragments of Hawaiian history," now set forth in this book.

W. D. W.

PRONUNCIATION

In reading Hawaiian words do not end a syllable with a consonant, and pronounce all vowels as if they were Italian or French.

$$a = a \text{ in father.}$$
$$e = e \text{ in they.}$$
$$i = i \text{ in pin.}$$
$$o = o \text{ in hold.}$$
$$u = oo \text{ in spoon.}$$

This is a fairly good rule for the pronunciation of all Polynesian words.

I

MAUI THE POLYNESIAN

AMONG the really ancient ancestors of the Hawaiian chiefs, Maui is one of the most interesting. His name is found in different places in the high chief genealogy. He belonged to the mist land of time. He was one of the Polynesian demi-gods. He was possessed of supernatural power and made use of all manner of enchantments. In New Zealand antiquity he was said to have aided other gods in the creation of man.

Nevertheless he was very human. He lived in thatched houses, had wives and children, and was scolded by the women for not properly supporting his family. Yet he continually worked for the good of men. His mischievous pranks would make him another Mercury living in any age before the beginning of the Christian era.

When Maui was born his mother, not caring for him, cut off a lock of her hair, tied it around him and cast him into the sea. In this way the name came to him, Maui-Tiki-Tiki, "Maui formed in the topknot."

The waters bore him safely. Jellyfish enwrapped him and mothered him. The god of the seas protected him. He was carried to the god's house and hung up in the roof that he might feel the warm air of the fire and be cherished into life.

When he was old enough he came to his relations while they were at home, dancing and making merry. Little Maui crept in and sat down behind his brothers. His mother called the children and found a strange child, who soon proved that he was her son. Some of the brothers were jealous, but the eldest addressed the others as follows:

"Never mind; let him be our dear brother. In the days of peace remember the proverb, 'When you are on friendly terms, settle your disputes in a friendly way; when you are at war, you must redress your injuries by violence.' It is better for us, brothers, to be kind to other people. These are the ways by which men gain influence—by labouring for abundance of food to feed others, by collecting property to give to others, and by similar means by which you promote the good of others."

Thus, according to the New Zealand story related by Sir George Grey, Maui was received in his home.

Maui's home in Hawaii was for a long time enveloped in darkness. According to some legends the skies pressed so closely and so heavily upon the earth that when the plants began to grow all the leaves were necessarily flat. According to other legends the plants had to push up the clouds a little, and thus the leaves flattened out into larger surface, so that they could better drive the skies back. Thus the leaves became flat and have so remained through all the days of mankind. The plants lifted the sky inch by inch until men were able to crawl about between the heavens and the earth, thus passing from place to place and visiting one another. After a long time Maui came to a woman and said: "Give me a drink from your gourd calabash and I will push the heavens higher." The woman handed the gourd to him. When he had taken a deep draught he braced himself against the clouds and lifted them to the height of the trees. Again he hoisted the sky and carried it to the tops of the mountains; then, with great exertion, he thrust it up to the place it now occupies. Nevertheless, dark clouds many times hang low along the great mountains and descend in heavy rains, but they dare not stay, lest Maui, the strong, come and hurl them so far away that they cannot come back again.

The Manahiki Islanders say that Maui desired to separate the sky from the earth. His father, Ru, was the supporter of the heavens. Maui persuaded him to assist in lifting the burden. They crowded it and bent it upward. They were able to stand with the sky resting on their shoulders. They heaved against the bending mass and it receded rapidly. They quickly put the palms of their hands under it, then the tips of their fingers, and it retreated farther and farther. At last, drawing themselves out to gigantic proportions, they pushed the entire heavens up to the very lofty position which they have ever since occupied.

On the island Hawaii, in a cave under a waterfall, dwelt Hina-of-the-fire, the mother of Maui.

From this home Maui crossed to the island Maui, climbed a great mountain, threw ropes made from fibres of plants around the sun's legs, pulled off many and then compelled the swift traveller of the heavens to go slowly on its way that men might have longer and better days.

Maui's home, at the best, was only a sorry affair. Gods and demi-gods lived in caves and small grass houses. The thatch rapidly rotted and required continual renewal. In a very short time the heavy rains beat through the decaying roof. The home was without windows or doors, save as low openings in the ends or sides allowed entrance to those willing to crawl through. Here Maui lived on edible roots and fruits and raw fish, knowing little about cooked food, for the art of fire-making was not yet known.

By and by Maui learned to make fire by rubbing sticks together.

A family of mud hens, worshipped by some of the Hawaiians in later years, understood the art of fire-making.

From the sea Maui and his brothers saw fire burning on a mountain side but it was always put entirely out when they hastened to the spot.

Maui proposed to his brothers that they go fishing, leaving him to watch the birds. But the Alae counted the fishermen and refused to build a fire for the hidden one who was watching them. They said among themselves, "There are three in the boat and we know not where the other one is, we will make no fire to-day."

So the experiment failed again and again. If one or two remained or if all waited on the land there would be no fire—but the dawn which saw the four brothers in the boat, saw also the fire on the land.

Finally Maui rolled some kapa cloth together and stuck it up in one end of the canoe so that it would look like a man. He then concealed himself near the haunt of the mud-hens, while his brothers went out fishing. The birds counted the figures in the boat and then started to build a heap of wood for the fire.

Maui was impatient—and just as an old bird began to select sticks with which to make the flames he leaped swiftly out and caught her and held her prisoner. He forgot for a moment that he wanted the secret of fire-making. In his anger against the wise bird his first impulse was to taunt her and then kill her for hiding the secret of fire.

But the bird cried out: "If you are the death of me—my secret will perish also—and you cannot have fire."

Maui then promised to spare her life if she would tell him what to do.

Then came a contest of wits. The bird told the demi-god to rub the stalks of water plants together. He guarded the bird and tried the plants. Then she told him to rub reeds together—but they bent and broke and he could make no fire. He twisted her neck until she was half dead—then she cried out: "I have hidden the fire in a green stick."

Maui worked hard but not a spark of fire appeared. Again he caught his prisoner by the head and wrung her neck, and she named a kind of dry wood. Maui rubbed the sticks together but they only became warm. The twisting process was resumed—and repeated until the mud-hen was almost dead—and Maui had tried tree after tree. At last Maui found fire. Then as the flames rose he said: "There is one more thing to rub." He took a fire stick and rubbed the top of the head of his prisoner until the feathers fell off and the raw flesh appeared. Thus the Hawaiian mud-hen and her descendants have ever since had bald heads, and the Hawaiians have had the secret of fire-making.

Maui was a great discoverer of islands. Among other groups he "fished up from the ocean" New Zealand and the Hawaiian Islands with a magic hook. One by one he pulled them to himself out of the deep waters. He discovered them.

Thus Maui raised the sky, lassoed the sun, found fire and made the earth habitable for man.

II

MAUI SEEKING IMMORTALITY

THE story of Maui seeking immortality for the human race is one of the finest myths in the world. For pure imagination and pathos it is difficult to find any tale from Grecian or Latin literature to compare with it. In Greek and Roman fables gods suffered for other gods, and yet none were surrounded with such absolutely mythical experiences as those through which the demi-god Maui of the Pacific ocean passed when he entered the gates of death with the hope of winning immortality for mankind. The really remarkable group of legends which cluster around Maui is well concluded by the story of his unselfish and heroic battle with death.

The different islands of the Pacific have their hades, or abode of the dead. Sometimes the tunnels left by currents of melted lava running toward the west are the passages into the home of departed spirits. In Samoa there are two circular holes among the rocks at the west end of the island Savaii. These are the entrances to the underworld for chiefs and people. The spirits of those who die on the other islands leap into the sea and swim around the land from island to island until they reach Savaii. Then they plunge down into their heaven or their hades.

There is no escape from death. The natives of New Zealand say: "Man may have descendants but the daughters of the night strangle his offspring"; and again: "Men make heroes, but death carries them away."

Maui once said to the goddess of the moon: "Let death be short. As the moon dies and returns with new strength, so let men die and revive again."

But she replied: "Let death be very long, that man may sigh and sorrow. When man dies let him go into darkness, become like earth, that those he leaves behind may weep and wail and mourn."

"Maui did not wish men to die but to live forever. Death appeared degrading and an insult to the dignity of man. Man ought to die like the moon which dips in the life-giving waters of Kane and is renewed again, or like the sun, which daily sinks into the pit of night and with renewed strength rises in the morning."

The Hawaiian legends say that Maui was slain in a conflict with some of the gods. The New Zealand legends give a more detailed account of his death.

Maui sought the home of Hine-nui-te-po—the guardian of life. He heard her order her attendants, the brightest flashes of lightning, to watch for

any one approaching and capture all who came
walking upright as a man.   He crept past the attendants on hands and feet, found the place of life,
stole some of the food of the goddess and returned
home.   He showed the food to his brothers and
friends and persuaded them to go with him into
the darkness of the night of death.   On the way he
changed them into the form of birds.   In the evening they came to the house of the goddess on an
island long before fished up from the seas.

Maui warned the birds to refrain from making
any noise while he made the supreme effort of his
life.   He was about to enter upon his struggle for
immortality.   He said to the birds: "If I go into
the stomach of this woman do not laugh until I
have gone through her, and come out again at her
mouth; then you can laugh at me."

His friends said: "You will be killed."   Maui
replied: "If you laugh at me when I have only
entered her stomach I shall be killed, but if I have
passed through her and come out of her mouth I
shall escape and Hine-nui-te-po will die."

His friends called out to him: "Go then.   The
decision is with you."

Hine was sleeping soundly.   The sunlight had
almost passed away and the house lay in quiet
gloom.   Maui came near to the sleeping goddess.
Her large fishlike mouth was open wide.   He put
off his clothing and prepared to pass through the
ordeal of going to the hidden source of life, tear it

out of the body of its guardian and carry it back
with him to mankind. He stood in all the glory of
savage manhood. His body was splendidly marked
by the tattoo-bones, and now well oiled shone and
sparkled in the last rays of the setting sun.

He leaped through the mouth of the enchanted
one and entered her stomach, weapon in hand, to
take out her heart, the vital principle which he knew
had its home somewhere within her being. He
found immortality on the other side of death. He
turned to come back again into life when suddenly
a little bird laughed in a clear, shrill tone and Great
Hine, through whose mouth Maui was passing,
awoke. Her sharp, obsidian teeth closed with a
snap upon Maui, cutting his body in the centre.
Thus Maui entered the gates of death, but was un-
able to return, and death has ever since been victor
over rebellious men. The natives have the saying:

"If Maui had not died he could have restored
to life all who had gone before him, and thus succeeded in destroying death."

Maui's brothers took the dismembered body and
buried it in a cave called Te-ana-i-hana. "The cave
dug out," possibly a prepared burial place.

Maui's wife made war upon the gods, and killed
as many as she could to avenge her husband's death.
One of the old native poets of New Zealand in
chanting the story to Mr. White said: "But
though Maui was killed his offspring survived.
Some of these are at Hawa-i-ki (Hawaii) and

some at Ao-tea-roa (New Zealand) but the greater part of them remained at Hawaiki. This history was handed down by the generations of our ancestors of ancient times, and we continue to rehearse it to our children, with our incantations and genealogies, and all other matters relating to our race."

> "But death is nothing new
> Death is, and has been ever since old Maui died
> Then Pata-tai laughed loud
> And woke the goblin-god
> Who severed him in two, and shut him in,
> So dusk of eve came on."
>
> —*Maori Death Chant.*

III

THE WATER OF LIFE *

"THE SELF-RELIANT DRAGON" is frequently mentioned in the oldest Hawaiian legends. This dragon was probably a very old crocodile worshipped as the ancestor goddess of the Hawaiian chief families.

She dwelt in one of the mysterious islands mentioned in the Hawaiian chants as Kua-i-Helani, "the Far-away Helani," lying in the ancient far western home of the Polynesians.

Iku was the chief. He had several sons. The youngest was Aukele-nui-a-Iku, Aukele the Great Son of Iku.

Aukele was a favorite of the Self-reliant Dragon. She gave him a large bamboo stick. Inside she placed an image of the god Lono, and also a magic leaf which could provide plenty of food for any one who touched the leaf to his lips. She put in a part of her own skin.

She said, "This skin is a cloak for you. If you lift it up against any enemies, they will fall to pieces as dust and ashes."

* This is one of the most ancient legends in Hawaiian annals.

They put all these treasures in the bamboo stick. Then the dragon taught the boy all kinds of magic power.

The brothers, who were great warriors, determined to sail away, find a new land and conquer it by fighting. Aukele persuaded them to take him. Then he sent one to get the stick he had brought from the dragon pit which was near the sea.

After a long time on the sea all their food was gone and they were starving and lying in the bottom of the boat. Aukele fed them from the leaf which he touched to their lips.

Some days passed and Aukele said, "To-morrow we will come to a land where a woman is the ruler. Let me tell why we journey."

They said, "Did you build this boat, and have you its chant?"

He said: "We must not call this a boat for war, but of discovery, to find new land."

The chiefess of that land looked out and saw a boat in the ocean, and sent some birds to see what the boat was doing and learn whether it was a war canoe, or a travelling boat. The birds went out, and Aukele wanted his brothers to say it was a travelling boat. The birds asked and the brothers said: "This is a war canoe." The birds went away. Aukele took up the bamboo stick and threw it in the sea, and leaped in after it. The brothers threw the cloak of Aukele on the beach. The chiefess found the cloak and shook it toward the boat, then threw it away. The brothers broke into small dust and were destroyed. The boat and the brothers sank to the bottom of the sea.

Aukele swam to the beach, pulled up his stick, found his cloak and lay down under a tree and slept. A watchdog came out, and smelled the man, and barked.

The chiefess called two women, and told them to see who it was, and if they found any one, kill him. They came down and the god of Aukele awakened him, and told him the names of the women.

The women came and he greeted them. They were ashamed because he had found their names, and one said to the other, "What can we give him for naming us?" The other said, "We will let him be the husband of our ruler." So they came and sat down by him, and they talked lovingly together and he won their hearts.

The women told him that they had been sent to kill him, but that they would say they did not find him; then other messengers would be sent. They went home and told the chiefess: "We went to the precipice; there was no one there. Then to the forest and the sea. There was no one there. Perhaps the dog made a mistake."

The chiefess turned the dog out again; at once there was more barking. She told her bird brothers to go and look over the land. Lono saw them and said; "Here is another death day for us. I will tell you who these birds are. When they come you say their names quickly and welcome them." So he did. They wondered how he knew their names. This knowledge gave him power over them and they could not harm him. The birds also thought they would have to offer their ruler as a wife to this wonderful stranger. They went back to their sister and told her they had found a husband for her. This pleased her. She sent them after Aukele. He told them he would go by and by.

Lono said to Aukele, "Death has partly passed, but more trouble lies before us. When you go up do not sit down or enter the house. Stand at the door. First these two women will come. If they say 'Aloha' it is all right. The dog will come and will try to kill you. When he has passed by, the brothers will come. The food they make and put in old calabashes, do not eat. See if the calabash has anything growing in its cracks. You will find new calabashes scattered over the ground. Food and fish and water are inside. Eat from these."

He made ready to go, and went up to the house, and stood by the door. The two women said "Aloha" and called to him to come in, but he would not enter. The dog ran out, opened her mouth and tried to bite Aukele through the magic cloak. The dog became ashes. The chiefess saw the dog was dead and was very sorry because he was the watchman for her land.

The brothers came to him with food which they had put in moss-covered calabashes. He never touched it. It was the death food. He went to a place where green calabash vines were growing, took a calabash, shook it, broke it, opened it and found good food inside.

Then they lived as man and wife. The chiefess had been a cannibal but at this time stopped eating men. Soon a son was born.

After a time the bird brothers taught Aukele how to leap into the air and fly as a bird.

The chiefess told her brothers to go away into the heavens and find her father, Ku-waha-ilo, a cannibal god. He was also the father of Pele, the goddess of volcanic fire. They must tell him that she had given all her treasures to her husband— stars, lands, and seas. She told them to take her husband to see the father.

They flew away, Aukele flying faster than the others. The father saw him and thought his daughter was dead. He said, "She is the watchman for my land, and no man could come here if she were alive," and he was angry.

Lono told Aukele to put on his magic cloak that now covered him from head to foot. Then he understood there must be a battle. The cannibal father made fire, called Kuku-ena (the lightning); then Ikuwa, a stone crashing like thunder.

The lightning and the crashing stone were struck by the cloak and rattled into ashes, cracking and breaking, reverberating, sounding like a drum.

The bird brothers saw the fire and heard the thunder. They were far behind Aukele. They saw the lightning and the thunder defeated. After the battle, they all came before their father and told him that the daughter was well and this was her husband.

After this flight to a cannibal land and this victory over the cannibal god, Aukele returned to his wife.

After a time the ghosts of his brothers appeared to him and reminded him of their grave in the sea.

Aukele was very sorry and ate nothing for days. His wife, with great sympathy, told him if he had strength enough to find the living water of Kane he could still restore his brothers. He was encouraged and ate. He asked what path he should take to find the land of the water of life. She made a straight line toward the East, the sunrise, and told him to fly straight, not swerving to either side.

He took his bamboo stick with all his aid inside and put it under his arm, put on his magic cloak, and said "Aloha." A long time passed.

He thought he was flying in a straight line, but one arm became tired because the stick was under it. He changed the stick, and this moved his direction. His god saw this and told him he was leaving the straight line and was flying to some other place. There was fire far below. All the people had fled except one. The god said, "Let us go straight till we come to that one; then you catch him and hold him fast. We shall have life." This was the moon, who was an ancestress of his wife. The moon had been cooking food. She arose to take up her food and get ready to go. But Aukele caught her, held her and ate her food. She thus became thin—a new moon—and the traveller gained strength to return to his home.

Aukele thought he would try again, according to his wife's line. She made a line from the door of the house toward the sunrise, and warned him. He flew straight a long time until he found a strange land with a deep pit lined with trees and wonderful plants. At the bottom was the spring of the water of life. He leaped down upon the back of a watchman on the edge of the pit, who had been put there by the guardian to kill any one coming after the water. He tried to shake Aukele off, saying: "Who are you? What do you mean, O proud man? My grandchild, the brother of Pele, never got on my back. Who are you?" He gave his name and ancestors, and told the watchman he had come for the water of life for his brothers. The watchman said: "Go straight out from where I stand. Do not turn to the side or you will strike bamboo which will make a great noise, and my grandchild, Pele's brother, will hear and will cover the water tight, and you cannot get it."

So Aukele flew and leaped straight on the second watchman, who told him not to go to the left or he would strike the lama trees (very hard wood, used for building houses for the gods). These trees would make a great noise and the guardian would cover the water tight and he could not get it.

He flew to another watchman, who told him to go straight to the bottom of the pit. "There a blind woman will be sitting. Look at the place where she is cooking bananas. She will take them one by one. You eat all her bananas. Then she will become angry and throw ashes. If she throws on the right side, you must fly to the left. Watch if she strikes with a stick, then run quickly, sit in her lap, and tell her who you are."

When he had done all these things and all attempts to kill him had failed, Aukele made the old blind woman lie down under a cocoanut tree. He got two young cocoanuts and told her to turn her eyes toward the sky. He dropped the cocoanuts in her eyes. She wept sorely because of the pain. He told her to rub the water out of her eyes and not cry. She did so, and said: "I can see you." He came down from the tree and she told him what he must do to get the water of life: "Go and break the stem of a water plant, and near it a bush with white flowers. Bring them to me." This he did and laid the plants before her. She squeezed the water from the plants into a cup, took charcoal and other things and mixed them together until black; then she painted Aukele's hands very black, like the hands of the brother of Pele. His hands were black, and those watching the water of life would look at the hands reaching for water and make no mistake. They would tightly cover up the water if a white hand came down. "Wait until the guardian god is asleep and the servants are preparing drink for him when he should awake. Then go to the door and one will give you some water. The first will be dirty water; throw it away. Put your hand down again. They will give you another calabash of water. This will be the living water of Kane; take it."

He went down and put his hand in for the water. The watchman handed out a calabash of dirty water. He threw it away and again thrust his black hand down the pit.

The watchman gave him a calabash of the pure water of life.

He flew rapidly along the path to the outside world. In his haste he struck the leaves of the groves of trees and the noise was that of strong winds thrashing the branches and leaves back and forth, up and down. The sound swept through the land of the water of life like rolling thunder.

The brother of Pele and his servants awoke and followed, but he fled through the heavens to the place where the ghosts of his brothers lay in the sunken ship by the home of the goddess of the sea.

They all went down to the sea. The chiefess told her husband to pour the water of life in his hand. She put her fingers in the water and sprinkled drops over the sea.

Out in the ocean under the moving surface was a boat, its mast coming up through the waves. In a little while they saw men standing in the boat. These were the brothers of Aukele. After the welcome, he gave them lands and homes.

In that strange far-off land of the ancestors—the mysterious "Floating Island"—the "Hidden Island of Kane," it is said they still live under the rule of their younger brother.

Aukele thought he would like to see his parents once more, so he went to the far-away Helani—but the land was desolate. The parents were gone, the people had disappeared, the houses had all decayed, and the land was covered with a forest.

Only a dragon was left—one of the family of the "Self-reliant Dragon." He discovered her body fast in the coral reef near the shore. He thought she was dead, but he stood up and stamped with full strength and broke the coral so that the dragon was free. He saw the body moving, but the dragon was very weak and near death.

He was sorry for her, remembering that it was by the aid of dragon powers he had gone into the heavens and from the deep pit of the skies secured the water of life. Therefore he provided food and gave new life to the dragon.   He asked about his parents and their gods, and the desolation of the land.

The dragon told him how the entire household of gods, dragons and men had found a new home, in the Islands of Oahu and Hawaii.   She told how "the child adopted or brought up by the gods," and the Maiden of the Golden Clouds, had been taken by the Self-reliant Dragon to Oahu, and how all the rest had gone, leaving her as a guard in the old land of his birth and childhood.

Aukele went back to the legendary land, the "Hidden Island of Kane," and there lived among the ghost gods who welcome the dead as they escape from wandering over the islands and fly by the path of the sunset back to the home of the most distant ancestors—the mysterious lands in the skies of the western seas.

Here he and his brothers are high chiefs of the au-makuas, the ghost gods of Hawaii, who wait to welcome and give peace to the spirits of the dead.

IV

A VIKING OF THE PACIFIC

H ISTORY is frequently legendary. That historian is incompetent who deliberately ignores tradition and fable. A nation founded in the sunlight of civilisation cannot have a legendary past, but it must depend many times upon the cloudy memory of individuals. Legends are the indistinct memories of nations, and are of real value when there is any opportunity for comparison. Early Norse history was told in song legends. The sagas of the Vikings are rivalled in some measure by the meles of the Hawaiians. The Hawaiians have both *the chant—the mele,* and the *tradition—the olelo.* From these come Hawaiian ancient history. The Vikings, "sea kings," as they are often named, the "wickel-ings," as Froude calls them, the men who sailed out from the "vicks," the fjords of the Scandinavian coast, were brave mariners. They swept the European coast; they infested Mediterranean waters; they found the North Atlantic islands. They made themselves at home in Sneeland (Snowland), now Iceland and Greenland. They named the countries newly discovered after their own fancies, as Flatland, Woodland, and Vinland, for Newfoundland, Nova Scotia and Massachusetts, respectively.

The Polynesian folklore abounds in stories of remarkable men, bold expeditions, stirring adventures and voyages to far-off lands. The Vikings of the Pacific gave to their foreign lands the names by which these lands were then known, and by which they are known to-day.

In the long Hawaiian chant of Kumu Honua, "the first created," there is a part devoted to Hawaii-loa, the first sea-king of the Polynesians. He is reported as making long journeys and discovering the Hawaiian Islands. Besides this chant there are many legends and references which make him an important ancestor among Hawaiians, an ancestor of islands rather than of families. He lived in the "land of the handsome or golden god, Kane." To the north lay the land Ulu-nui or "the Great Ulu," possibly Ur of Chaldea. His home was near the "green precipiced paradise" of Hawaiian legend, the place where the water of life gave forth healing even for the dead.

Hawaii-loa was a noted fisherman. He launched out into deep waters. He fished for new worlds and found them. From the Great Ulu to Java, from Java to Jilolo, and from Jilolo far out into the eastern Pacific, Hawaii-loa sailed. His relative, Ti-i, also launched out into the deep seas. Ti-i went almost directly east from the old home, and found the Society Islands. These he made his home, according to the Society Island legends, becoming the creator of the islands.

Hawaii-loa sailed to the northeast, following "Iao," Jupiter, as the morning star. Iao was a favorite guiding star among the Hawaiians. Five of the planets were known by the sea-rovers. The planets were called "Na Hoku hele"—"the going stars." Mars was known as "Hoku ula," "the red star." "Na hoku paa" were "the fastened stars, immovable in the heavens." The name "Iao" is given to one of the mountains of the Island of Maui.

Hawaii-loa found the fire islands—the islands somewhat like the old Java home, luxuriant and volcanic. He named the large island Hawa-i-i— "the little or the burning Java."

The large island was full of delight to the bold navigator, and he determined to bring his family to this new land for their permanent home. He took them from "the land where his forefathers dwelt before him." He sailed through the "dotted sea," the sea with many islands lying near his old ancestral home, "the rainy Zaba"—the modern Zaba or Saba of the Arabian seacoast—from which his own name, "Hawa," is easily derived. On his journey back and forth he passed through a sea which delighted his heart as a fisherman—"a sea where the fishes run." He must have found excellent deep-sea fishing. He crossed the "many-

coloured ocean" and the "sky-blue sea." He rev-
elled in the beauty of the sun rising and setting in
glorious colours on the restless waves. On he
sailed with his family until he came to Hawaii—
"the burning Java," the land of volcanoes and
earthquakes and of luxuriant valleys and fertile
seacoasts.

Fornander suggests that Hawaii is derived from
Java and Java from the Arabian Saba.

Evidently a Polynesian chief of high rank gathered a number of adherents or members of his
tribe, and sailed eastward over the Pacific, about
the beginning of the Christian era. His descendants, or at least such portion of his family as did
not follow him on his voyage, seem to have moved
from Java to the Molucca Islands and settled in
Jilolo.

It is said that after he brought his family to
Hawaii, new islands sprang out of the sea, well
wooded and well watered. These he divided
among his children.

When the later sea-rovers came to Hawaii, possibly in the fifth or sixth century, they found the
islands already inhabited by people of their own
race, and yet apparently without a chief—probably
a servant class. If we sift the legends and then
assume that in the course of three or four hundred years the family of the chief, Hawaii-loa, became extinct in Hawaii, leaving only the servants
on the islands, we have at least a probable expla-

nation of the coming of the so-called little people, or fairies, from the Southern Pacific to Hawaii.

The South Pacific islanders called their servants, or laborers, the Manahune people.

The fairies were known in the Hawaiian legends as the Menehunes. Sometimes they were credited with powers like the gnomes of old England. They were supposed to work only at night. A very ancient stone water-wall along the side of one of the swift-flowing Hawaiian rivers has no tradition or history save that the Menehune people built it in one night. Another very ancient stone wall around a large fish pond is referred to the Menehunes, who did not finish their work in one night, therefore the wall has always been incomplete. So also some of the most ancient temples were referred to the mysterious midnight labors of this people.

One of the legends states that a priest desired to carry the Menehune people across the long stretch of ocean between the foreign lands and the Island of Oahu, therefore "he stretched out his hands to the farthest bounds of Tahiti and over him the Menehunes—the servants—crossed to Oahu."

It was this same sorcerer-priest who saw the sun die and the earth become dark. He leaped across to the foreign land, caught the sun before it was buried, brought it back to Hawaii and placed it in the heavens, where it has been ever since. These are simply graphic descriptions of an eclipse, and also of a chief who carried his common people—his servants—with him across the waters. The presence of this servant class in the very ancient times is unquestioned.

Chiefs coming later found this servant class which readily accepted new rulers.

Hawaii-loa—"the Great Hawaii"—may well be considered both a founder of the Polynesian race and the first settler of the Hawaiian Islands. Brave lover of the sea and founder of nations, Hawaii-loa deserves first place among the Vikings of the Pacific.

V

LEGENDARY HOME OF THE POLYNESIANS

THE Hawaiians, like the native residents of many other groups of islands in the Pacific Ocean, have not taken kindly to the European names tacked upon their doorposts by the sailors who discovered them. This is very fortunate for those who desire to gather together the facts out of which to weave a connected history of Polynesia.

It is also fortunate that the language spoken in the groups so widely diffused over the Pacific Ocean, has the same common structure, with only such differences as may be resolved into dialects.

The Tahitian, Samoan, New Zealander, and Hawaiian, though thousands of miles apart, are members of one family, and require but a short period to acquire the faculty of a free exchange of ideas.

Students find a slight difficulty in the different spellings which different voyagers have given to the native words according to the way in which they heard the sounds—for instance, "Hawaii" was "Owyhee" in the days of Captain Cook.

This difficulty was not overcome when the Polynesian dialects were reduced to writing by the many missionaries to the different parts of the Pacific Ocean. It was impossible to adopt a uniform method. In some places "h" was used, in others "f" and "l" or "r" or "k," as in the Hawaiian word "aloha"—which in other island groups was "alofa" and "aloofa," "aroha," "kaoha," "akaaroa," all meaning "friendship."

In attempting to trace the place of origin of the Hawaiians and other Polynesians it is absolutely necessary to take into account this phonetic difficulty.

Fornander gives the following list of island groups with the various methods of using the word Hawaii:

> Hawaii—Hawa-i-i.
> Tahiti—Hawa-i-i.
> Samoa—Sawa-i-i or Sava-i-i.
> New Zealand—Hawa-iki.
> Marquesas—Hawa-iki.
> Raro Tonga—Awa-iki.
> Tonga—Haba-i.

Hawaii in some form of the word is the most universally used name among all the Polynesians as the place for their ancestral home.

The name of the Hawaiian Islands is taken from this mythological name. So also is the Savaii of the Samoan Islands. So also the small island

Hawaiki in Lake Rotorua of New Zealand, where the New Zealand legends say the ancestors of the Maoris placed the relics which they brought with them from their ancestral Hawaiki when they settled in New Zealand. In far eastern Tahiti is a place on Raiatea, the island now known as Opoa. Its ancient and sacred name was Hawaii.

Some writers have thought that Samoa might be the center of dispersion to the other Pacific islands, but the Samoan dialect is very corrupt, its legends are fragmentary, and its history of sea rovers seems to lack a sufficient similarity of names with the migrators from the original home to allow this supposition to have very great weight.

It is also interesting to note that the Hawaiian Islands do not have a good foundation for any claim to be the original centre of dispersion, although many of the most ancient legends of Hawaii and of New Zealand are the same. There is abundance of proof of a common origin, but not sufficient to found any claim for Hawaiian parentage.

Ellis, writing in 1830 concerning the Tahitians and inhabitants of neighbouring islands, says:

"A tradition stated that the first inhabitants of these islands originally came from a country in the direction of the setting sun, to which several names were given. Pigs and dogs were brought from the West."

In the Hawaiian Islands the point from which

the ancient voyages sailed away to visit the other groups of islands of the Pacific was off the western coast of the island of Maui and was called Ke-ala-i-kahiki, The Path to Tahiti. They might ultimately sail eastward to Tahiti or to the Marquesas Islands, but they started toward the home of their ancestors, westward. They called their vikings— *Ka-poe-holo-kahiki,* The People Sailing to Tahiti. Tahiti at last meant any distant or foreign group of islands, although individual names of islands are used in the chants—such as Bolabola and Upolu.

The Hawaiian said that, *ke alo,* the face or front of an island, was toward the west. The back, *ke kua,* was toward the east. This, as Fornander says, was "because the ancestors of the islanders came from the west originally."

The students of Polynesian legends are practically united in ascribing the Hawaii of mythology to some place west of all the islands.

Early writers on the origin of the Polynesians took it for granted that these ancestors were Malays. Certain words and names among both Malays and Polynesians were similar, but later study has convinced the vast majority of students that this theory is not true. It is now believed that the Polynesians came to the island groups from the neighbourhood of the straits of Sunda, where they had their home for a long time. The fierce Malay tribes descended upon them and scattered them in all directions over the seas. A trace of the remnants of this dispersion is found even among the mixed elements of the people of Japan. Another trace is found in Madagascar, while the great body of the storm-tossed people took possession of the middle and southeastern islands of the Pacific.

Hon. Edward Tregear, of New Zealand, writing about the *original* home of the Polynesians, thinks that their first residence was either India or Central Asia, from whence they passed through India, there making a stay of some time. Then they journeyed to the Malay archipelago, residing there many generations until driven out by the Malays. This is the original Hawa-iki from which Polynesia was first settled, expeditions probably passing out to the far distant island groups. Then lastly came the canoe voyagers—the rovings of the vikings of the Pacific which in New Zealand meant a new peopling of the land of the "long white cloud," and to the Hawaiians and Tahitians and other islands almost two centuries of adventurous sea roving.

The late Hon. S. Percy Smith, Minister of Native Affairs in New Zealand, traces the Polynesians from Aryan connection in Asia Minor and Western Europe to India, Malayasia and thence to the scattered islands of the Pacific.

Max Muller calls attention to the use of the word *Av-iki* by both Brahmins and Buddhists as the name of their "hades."

Hawa-iki was the name of the place from which

the Polynesians came and about which they talked in their most ancient stories. This other world became mysterious as the ages passed by until at last Hawa-iki meant the place to which the spirits of the dead went, as well as the home from which their ancestors came. A journey to or from any of the Polynesian islands meant passing out of one world into another. The area of vision bounded by the horizon was the world in which the people lived. Passing out of sight over the waters was breaking through the wall dividing one world from another. The idea that Hawa-iki was the home of the ghosts could very easily be derived from the other world beyond the shining wall of the sky into which any one sailing out of sight of land might be forever lost.

The path into this other world—this Hawa-iki of the ancestors—was universally toward the west —the golden path of the setting sun.

VI

THE SONS OF KII

SOMETIME during the fifth or sixth century of the Christian era—according to estimates based on Hawaiian genealogies—two brothers, Ulu and Nanaulu, came to the Hawaiian Islands and established a dynasty of high chiefs. Their father was Kii, a king in the Southern Pacific Islands. Tahiti, the chief island of the Society group, furnishes the only ancient king of that name. We have the additional fact that in Hawaiian legends the place to which Hawaiian Vikings frequently sailed for centuries was usually Kahiki or Tahiti, the old home of the family of ruling chiefs.

It has been suggested that Ulu remained in the southern islands and that Nanaulu alone found his way to Hawaii; but the frequent use of the name Ulu in the genealogies of the chiefs of the two large islands, Hawaii and Maui, would support the position taken in the story that follows—that the brothers, sailing together, found Hawaii.

*　　　*　　　*　　　*　　　*

Two strong young men, about six feet in stature, were hastening together along a mountain spur leading down to the harbour of Papeete. They had met but a short time before, one coming around the base of the turreted crags of an extinct volcano known as "La Diademe"—The Diadem, or crown of Tahiti. The other had left his house in the hills from which the beautiful river of the Vai-ta-piha valley takes its source. They had given each other the universal Polynesian greeting—"Love to you," with the reply, "Love indeed."

Soon they came to the seashore where a long boat, the waa of Ulu, had been built. Large crowds of natives were watching the workmen as the stone adzes rang for the last time on the boarded-up sides of the boat.

As the two young chiefs drew near they saw a small company of solemn, dignified men, evidently of high rank, emerge from the door of a large grass house and march slowly to the side of the long boat.

A trumpet shell was sounded. The people fell with their faces toward the ground. Another blast, and there could be seen a number of gigantic slaves coming from the door of a stone temple not far away. Each slave was leading a prisoner. In a few minutes they surrounded the boat. Two prisoners were held at the prow of the boat, two at the stern, four along the boat sides and others in a line extending to the beach.

A priest stepped forth from the little company of leaders. In a strong and yet monotonous tone he began a chant of praise of Kii and his sons. He sang of the boat building and the protecting care of the gods.

He chanted the charms which would control the action of the gods of the seas over which the boats might sail. He invoked the gods of the home land to make friendly the gods of any new country to which the sailors might go. He pleaded for the acceptance of the human sacrifice about to be made to the gods.

Executioners with sharp-edged clubs of heavy hardwood then struck down the prisoners as the boat was rushed to the sea.

Human sacrifices at the launchings of the canoes of chiefs were not at all unusual, but the two young chiefs from the mountains had never before known such wholesale slaughter. The importance of the plans of the high chiefs was made evident by this large human sacrifice. The new boat of the king's son, Ulu, was evidently destined for some very important expedition.

"E Taunoa," cried a chief to the two latest arrivals, calling one of them by the name of his district. "Make haste or you will be too late to hear the voice of the king."

"How is it, Taunoa," said another, "that you, a chief of Nanaulu, should be present at the call of Kii in the interest of Ulu?"

Taunoa replied: "We shall soon see Nanaulu with a cloud of boats. I was sent to announce his coming to his father, the king. His heart is with his brother Ulu in the observance of the plans of Kii. I found this young chief of Vai-ta-piha on his way hither, and made him my companion. Take me at once to Kii, the king."

Okela, the chief who had called to Taunoa, at once preceded the crowd thronging hastily behind, giving Taunoa the post of honour after Okela. As they approached the dignified high chiefs they all prostrated themselves to the ground except Okela and Taunoa.

Taunoa drew from under his cloak a feathery frond of the cocoanut, and raising it above his head, asked for an interview with the king.

The trumpeter with his large pu or conch shell sounded the call of the coming of the king. Trumpet shells responded from the temple and from the king's residence. A terrific beating of drums followed, the people fell upon their faces; even the high chiefs prostrated themselves. Only the messenger from Nanaulu remained partially upright.

From the king's house came the royal retinue. King Kii was borne on the shoulders of a stalwart slave, supported by two other slaves, while ranks of trusted chiefs walked by his side. Following the king, riding in the same way upon the shoulders of slaves, was Ulu, the king's son, surrounded also by his chosen chiefs.

To the king Taunoa at once presented his tuft

of the cocoanut and was ordered to give his message.

"O King," he said, "Nanaulu, the high chief, your son, has heard of the boat of Ulu and your purpose of sending Ulu upon a mysterious mission. Nanaulu, the elder brother, was the kahu (caretaker) of Ulu in the days past. He desires to still stand by his brother's side and care for him in the place of Kii, the royal father. He has searched the forests of the sharp-peaked mountain and has fashioned a boat, the Mano-nui (great shark), and soon expects to come to Papeete with a royal fleet to do honour to the king, his father."

The king had turned his eyes for a moment toward Ulu and had caught the joy flashing from his eyes when he heard of his brother's speedy coming, then, looking down upon Taunoa, who had prostrated himself as soon as his message was delivered, simply said:

"Your message gives joy," and then was borne into the midst of the group of high chiefs.

The king's herald then made proclamation:

"Where are you, O chiefs? Where are you, O nobles of Tahiti? Where are you, O servant people? For the message is to all, from the highest to the lowest. Listen, O men of Tahiti, to the will of Kii, your king.

"It is his wish that Ulu, his son, should sail toward the west and should find the land of our fathers. He will have many companions, but these will be selected from only the most worthy.   His prophets and priests, his teachers, have already been chosen.   But now choice must be made of chiefs and warriors and common people.   Two days will be given you for rest.   On the third day the king and his high chiefs will be judges of wrestling contests.   On the fourth day will be struggles in the surf; or, if the sea gods are not propitious the chiefs will contest on the hillsides and in the games of physical strength.   On the fifth day there will be the exercise with the spears and clubs.   The skill and strength of the Tahitians will be manifest during these days."

Then followed such a scene of unbridled revelry as could occur only in a land given up to physical pleasures and passions.   Feasting and the heiva dance and drinking kava occupied the time of the common people.

The chiefs gave themselves up to gambling and rioting until the night was wearied with their excesses and the new day sent the revellers to needed rest wherever any tree or grass house afforded even a little shade.

As the afternoon of the first day began to cast its long shadows, a large fleet of hundreds of canoes filled the entrance to Papeete Bay.   They were preceded by a very large war canoe with a prow shaped into a rude resemblance of a shark's head, with shark's teeth fastened in the open jaws.   The body of the boat was of polished wood, well oiled.   The

multitude of canoes following were painted and
stained with as many brilliant dyes as possible.
Not a torn or weather-beaten sail hung by the
masts.   Sails of dyed kapa cloth and woven matting, new and beautifully painted, had been made
ready long before, that Nanaulu's homecoming
might have no blot upon its impressive appearance.
As the large boat came near the shore the oarsmen leaped into the surf; chosen men from the
other canoes joined them.   Passing strong cords of
cocoanut fibre under the keel, they lifted the boat,
with several chiefs resting upon a small deck which
partially covered the canoe.   Then they bore the
great burden up the beach toward the grass house
of Kii.   Standing by the mast of the canoe was
Nanaulu, a chief of splendid physical appearance,
about thirty years of age, before whom all the people prostrated themselves as he was carried by.

Midway between the beach and the king's house
a young chief rushed down to meet Nanaulu.   As
he came near the canoe he leaped over the heads of
the bearers, landing on the deck by the side of
Nanaulu and catching the mast gracefully, steadied
himself for a moment and then, throwing his arms
around Nanaulu, began the loud Polynesian wailing, with which in sorrow or in joy alike they were
accustomed to greet one another.   This was Ulu,
the younger brother, not over twenty-five years old,
and his warm-hearted greeting of his elder brother,
who during his boyhood had been his steadfast

friend and caretaker, showed the deep love which bound them together. Ulu was of higher chief rank than his elder brother. Sons of Kii, they were nevertheless sons of different queens of unequal rank; therefore Nanaulu owed allegiance to his brother. After the wailing was over the boat was carried to the king's house, while the two brothers discussed plans. Nanaulu requested that his own retainers might be given an opportunity to contest in the games and athletic exercises of the coming days. To this his brother readily acceded.

Early in the morning of the next day the contests were opened by the chiefs of the various districts of Tahiti, who called their best wrestlers together and chose the champions to contest with other champions from other districts.

After the king had taken his place the ceremonies of the day were introduced by the royal ceremonial dance. Over a hundred chiefs, throwing aside their cloaks and putting on tall helmets making the average stature about eight feet and, taking slender, thin paddles, ranged themselves before the king in lines, and then passed through a series of gymnastic exercises, gracefully moving the paddles in exact harmony, at the same time changing their positions, passing in and out between one another, sometimes forming squares, circles and semi-circles. The music for the rhythmic motion was furnished by rude drums, upon which musicians beat time. The dance ended by two chiefs taking war clubs and, while in motion, keeping time with the drums, twirling the clubs and striking rapidly at each other, circling the clubs over each other's heads and yet avoiding all injury to one another.

One of the chiefs stepped to the centre of the open arena and began to chant:

> "I am the wrestler
> From the groves of Papeete,
> By the sea waters.
> Where are you, Opale,
> The great man! the strong man!
> Living by the rough waves
> Of Makavia?
> Come and fight with Makima."

The champion wrestler from Matavia Bay very slowly walked into the arena, trying to appear utterly oblivious of his antagonist. He looked into the sky, glanced along the sand, then shouted:

> "Where are you, Makima,
> The boastful little man,
> The weak in limb and arm?
> Where are you, Makima,
> Who dares to fight with Opale?"

It was the custom of the Polynesians to throw out a taunt in a half-shouting, defiant tone. Each combatant approached the other, trying to make the audience think that he considered his antagonist so far beneath his notice that he only needed to move his arm and the match would be over. Thus in lordly dignity they ignored each other until, standing side by side, each made a sudden movement as if expecting to find the other off his guard. In a moment there was a confused mass of squirming limbs and arms and writhing bodies. A cloud of sand obscured the struggle. For a time there was no motion, and people saw the champions bending around each other with strained muscles, neither having any advantage, but each apparently exerting all his strength to make the other give way in response to brute strength. Each endeavoured to learn the trick by which his antagonist would change the order of battle. The least loosening of muscles on the part of one was interpreted in a moment by the other, and neither one hastened to carry out a move which might place him at the other's mercy. It was a splendid exhibition of statuesque athletics. Doing his very best to prevent betrayal by any loosened grasp in any direction, Opale suddenly swept one foot with terrific force against his antagonist's leg, at the same time pulling him to one side; but the half second's unconscious loosening of the muscles preparatory to Opale's action gave Makima notice, and even as Opale's foot struck him, he raised the unbalanced chief and whirled him over his head, at the same time by a whirlwind motion preserving his own equilibrium. Opale lay for a moment unconscious, while Makima received the applause of the multitude.

Then followed match after match, sometimes interspersed with boxing. In the boxing contests severe blows were given until one of the boxers was stricken senseless to the earth or an arm was broken. Sometimes both wrestling and boxing contests resulted in the death of a chief. At such times the chief's retainers quietly carried away the body, while the shouts which greeted the victor filled the air. Such deaths were taken as incidental, and no wailing showed the grief of stricken friends.

In this way the forenoon passed, and at last a few noble chiefs, exquisite in the beauty of perfect muscular manhood, stood before the king, chosen to be the special bodyguard of Ulu in the mysterious journey of the coming days. In the afternoon the followers of Nanaulu were tested and a like bodyguard selected for this young prince.

During that night a heavy wind tossed the sea waves into foam, but as the morning broke the wind died away, leaving ideal surf waves rolling in from the far-off coral reef, through the harbour, up to the beach.

A number of chiefs, taking long boards, thinned and smoothed by stone knives and polished with the rough skin of the shark, swam far out into the ocean. There where the surf waves began to form as the tide rolled landward each chief turned his surf board to follow the tidal pathway. Canoes were stationed at the point from which the older chiefs had decided that the swimmers must start. Groups of ten or fifteen contestants were allowed to start together.   The rider with the swiftest and most skilfully managed surf board was chosen from each group.   Hundreds of natives having any kind of claim to chief's blood had presented themselves for this contest.

Some of the surf-riders contented themselves by simply lying on the board, endeavouring by skilful use of hand and foot to hasten their passage on the crest of the huge surf waves.   This was by no means an easy thing to do.   Success consisted in gaining on the surf.   Ordinarily many surf waves passed from beneath the surf-riders before they could complete the long distance over the sea.   To hang to a wave, cling to its white mane, to have such mastery over it as not to be thrown back to the next wave, was a trial of strength and judgment, and might easily bring the sought-for reward. These, of course, were the first to reach the shore.

Others pushed their boards rapidly through the first waves encountered.   Then, balancing the board on the crest of the largest inrolling waves, leaped to their feet, and standing upright guided the board by the swaying of their bodies, adjusting themselves to the changing forces of the surf. Sometimes a very skilful surf-rider would go through the motions of fighting a battle—throwing the javelin, pushing with a spear, striking with a war-club or stabbing with a dagger.   This was seldom attempted without an ignominious overthrow of board and rider as the undertow from the

beach struggled with the incoming surf.   Then the
acrobat received the jeers of the people as he and
his boat rolled under the foam.   A successful completion of such a ride marked a high degree of combined courage and training and judgment.   During the course of the entire test of the men of both
Ulu and Nanaulu only two men perfectly performed
this difficult task.   These were the two young
high chiefs Okela and Taunoa.   The highest hon-
ours for surf-riding were, however, given by all
to Vai-ta-piha, the inferior chief who had come to
the contest with Taunoa.

Soon after the group of riders in which he was
placed started shoreward a squall broke over them.
The surf ceased rolling for a few moments in con-
tinuous waves.   The boards and their riders were
thrown against and over one another.   Then a
large wave swept the confused and struggling company toward the beach.   Vai-ta-piha easily extri-
cated himself, and balanced upon his surf board
was about to dash to land, but he saw in front of
his board the body of an insensible chief roll from
between two boards and begin to sink.   In a second he leaped ahead of his board, caught the chief
with one hand and with the other secured the surf-
board floating by.   He drew the chief and himself
up until he rested upon the board.   Leaping to his
feet he held the body in his hands, balancing himself and guiding his frail craft until the wave was
about to take its final plunge upon the sand, when

he dropped off into the water and carried his burden to the massage or lomilomi women, who by skilful kneading of the body soon restored the injured chief to his friends. The unselfish rescue as well as the skill displayed in bringing the body to land, all in a few moments, won the approval of the judges.

The fourth day the chiefs rested and the common people gave an exhibition of their attainments, and a sufficient number of canoe-makers, house-builders, fishermen and other helpers were easily secured. These were to be the oarsmen of the expedition.

The fifth day brought a new order of contestants. Around Papeete Bay are some beautiful hills, with sloping, grassy sides. Here the chiefs gathered with sleds which were from six to twelve feet long. These were made by taking finely polished hardwood for runners, usually about twelve inches apart.

Long sticks were placed lengthwise over these runners and fastened tightly to cross pieces. Frequently a board was tied between the sticks and a piece of matting laid upon it for the benefit of the rider. Holes were bored through these boards with sharp-pointed bones or shells, and they were strongly tied to the runners.

The riders of shorter sleds would grasp the sticks along the edges, using them as handles, raise the sled and run along the brow of the hill, giving the sled a hard push down the declivity as they threw themselves flat on the narrow board. Sometimes this resulted in a mortifying overthrow of the rider at the first leap of the sled downward. The rider with the longer sled was content to push his sled rapidly a few feet and then dash down the hillside. The slides or paths for the sleds were so well worn that little ridges formed along the sides, sometimes keeping the sled in the path, and just as often catching a runner and causing an overthrow of the rider.

The slides were frequently well covered with cut grass or leaves. Often the chiefs preferred the carefully kept, grass-covered, smooth hillside where but few marks of sleds appeared.

This was an exciting and sometimes dangerous sport. Fearful velocities were sometimes attained. Sleds swerved against slight unevennesses almost imperceptible until struck by a runner on one side or the other. The sudden shock swept the sled out of its course against the sled or in the pathway of an opponent, and in a moment a confused mass of broken sleds and stunned riders would be dashed down the hillside. Many times a sled thus turned spilt its runner on one side. It was considered evidence of great skill when a rider instantaneously adjusted himself to a broken sled, kept it in its course and finally landed safely in the smooth plain below.

Where the slopes were sufficiently gradual some

of the chiefs chose the slower ride, but took it in a standing position, when the dangers would be intensified, a broken sled being accompanied by broken limbs or a broken neck.

During the day messengers of the chiefs competed for a place in the expedition. The contest required the men to go around the mountain which formed the larger part of the Island of Tahiti, usually a two days' journey, with allowance for a few hours' rest along the way. The first and second runners to win in this race were to go as the messengers of Ulu and Nanaulu.

The contests among the chiefs had resulted in the selection of a much larger number of chiefs than could possibly go with the two young princes. New trials of skill were instituted to sift out the least skilful or the most unlucky.

The first test applied was that of javelin throwing. The high chiefs had prepared for their own sport a long, smooth path, beaten down until it was hard as a rock. Here they were accustomed to throw heavy hardwood darts, which, sliding along the path, would either pass between two marks at a given distance from the thrower or sometimes strike a small stick set upright at the end of a straight line drawn along the centre of the path. This was called the Pakee or the play with the darts or javelins.

A second test was made along the same beaten track in the game called Ulu-maika. In this con-

By courtesy Paradise of the Pacific

SPEAR THROWING CONTEST

test were used circular stones, flat-sided, of different sizes, according to the pleasure of the contestants. The smaller stones were about an inch thick and about six inches in circumference. The larger maika-stones were frequently two inches thick and a foot and a half in circumference. The ordinary stone used by most of the chiefs was an inch thick and about ten inches in circumference. These stones were smoothed and polished to a very high degree.

Those who had stood the test of javelin-throwing were formed in line that each one might, without delay, step to the head of the track and roll his disc, pass on and permit another to take his place.

This trial was, by virtue of a suggestion of Nanaulu, made a triple test. The stone was to be rolled more than the ordinary distance, made to pass between two upright sticks, then between two more posts, and then some distance beyond strike a mark set up in the centre of the track. Those accomplishing the entire feat would not be required to stand further trial in order to secure the coveted membership in the expedition. Those passing the posts should be entitled to another trial. It was not very difficult to roll the stone between the posts, but very few were able to keep the disc in the centre of the track and strike the far-distant mark.

The spear-catching contest was instituted as one of the final struggles. A difficult condition was attached to this spear-catching. Six spears were to be hurled at once by six chiefs not over sixty feet distant from the catcher. He was required to catch or stop at least four of these spears, not permitting more than two to pass by him.

Thus the contests ended, and thus by a skilful use of Polynesian games companions were selected for the sons of Kii in their long journey to Hawaii.

The wives of the young princes and some of the chiefs and warriors and boatmen were given places by the side of their husbands.

So from Tahiti, in the long ago, a voyage of many days to many lands, through many strange experiences, was undertaken by brave men and women in a small fleet of the larger kind of Polynesian boats. So the sons of Kii sailed away toward the west to find the home from which their ancestors had come to found the dynasty of Tahitian kings which held rule over Tahiti until the white man controlled the beautiful islands of the Pacific. Instead of the original home of the Polynesians on the coast of Asia, the sons of Kii probably made their way to the new Hawaii and there founded two races of kings. The descendants of Ulu ruled the larger southern islands until overthrown in the eleventh century by Paao on the Island of Hawaii. The descendants of Nanaulu ruled the northern islands until a few years after Captain Cook discovered the Hawaiian group and called it "The Sandwich Islands."

VII

PAAO FROM SAMOA

K A-MEHA-MEHA is the chief name around which Hawaiian history gathers. It is the nimbus of a cloud of stories, legends and chants. Hawaiians never reckoned history by dates, but by genealogies—as did the Hebrews. They measured time not by the years but by the lives of men; not by the days passed, but by the deeds done. These genealogies formed the most essential part of Hawaiian literature. They proved the royal descent of the high chiefs.

When Ka-meha-meha became king of "The Rainbow Islands," his royal chant took the supreme place. Other genealogies lost their importance except as they blended in that of the great king. He traced his royal blood to Pili, "from a foreign land," and through Pili back to Wa-kea, a Polynesian chief of perhaps the second century; and thence back through a series of hero-gods to Kumu-Honua, "the first created." It is a remarkable genealogy and worthy of study.

In November, 1736, he was born in North Kohala, Hawaii. Pili had settled in North Kohala about thirty generations preceding. A quarter of a century is accepted as the average life of a generation. Pili, therefore, landed in Hawaii in the early part of the eleventh century.

The story of Pili depends upon another story which must be told first. In fact the Hawaiian traditions tell a great deal more about Paao, the founder of the high-priest family of Hawaii, than about Pili, the ancestor of kings.

Not far from the year 1100 A. D., two priest brothers were living on Upolu, one of the Samoan Islands. Lonopele, the elder, lived in one of the luxurious valleys opening upon the seacoast. Paao, the younger, was a seaman as well as a priest. He lived near the beach, where he kept a small fleet of canoes.

In some way bitter feeling arose between the two households, making them jealous and suspicious of each other. One day Lonopele came to the temple where his brother was making ready to sacrifice a sacred black hog.

"Where are you, O Paao," he cried, "that you prepare a sacrifice for the favour of the gods, when you do not watch your oldest boy?"

"What is your thought?" asked Paao.

"Some of my choice fruits, brought from Tahiti, are beginning to ripen; and each night Kaino, your son, creeps under the low branches, and gathers whatever is good."

"It is false!" angrily replied the father.

Theft was considered the greatest of crimes among the Polynesians.

"No! It is true. He is coming even now from his feast. If he touches my fruit again he shall die. It is tabu" (sacred).

"E! Kaino!" called the father.

The boy came near, evidently having just been eating.

"Have you taken fruit from Lonopele in the night?"

"No. I have fruit at home, but better are the baked dog and fish. I would not eat his fruit."

Lonopele became angry, and cried out: "May the god, Kanaloa, curse you and break your body into fragments, for your falsehood."

"Cut open my stomach, O my uncle, and I shall be proved innocent."

The ancient days had little of the modern care for children. Fathers and mothers readily gave away their babes, or slew them with their own hands. Pao determined to substitute his son for the sacrifice he was preparing, and thus prove his guilt or innocence. No trace of fruit was found in the body.

Lonopele bowed his head in shame and hastened away. When the flush of indignant anger had passed, Paao grieved over the body which lay decomposing upon the altar. The Hawaiian traditions say that after this act he determined to leave Upolu. He called together a few of his trusted friends and told them his purpose. They agreed to prepare their large canoes, and go with him, seeking the "Burning-Java," or Hawaii, somewhere toward the north.

The sides of the boats were to be built two or three feet higher. This was done by hewing boards with stone axes, and sewing them to each other through holes, drilled by bones, using cords of cocoanut fibre for thread. Thus canoes were prepared capable of carrying thirty to sixty persons.

Dried bananas, pigs, fish, and pounded taro were made ready.

One day Paao saw his brother's son coming near the boats.

In a fit of anger he rushed upon the boy and slew him.

Lonopele soon discovered the murder, and made war upon Paao.

Paao and his friends launched their canoes as fast as possible, placing in them their families and such provisions as were at hand. His warriors, defeated by Lonopele, hastened to the canoes, and shoved out into the deep waters.

The battle was evidently fierce, for the legends say that some of the prophet friends who could not escape to their canoes, leaped from the precipitous cliffs to "fly" to the boats, and were dashed to pieces on the rocks below. Lonopele probably drove them over the brink of a precipice. One of the priest-friends leaped into the water, calling for Paao to return and rescue him. "Not so," answered Paao, "we have left the shore. It would be an evil omen to turn back. We will wait for you where we are." The legends say, "The priest flew like a bird to the canoes" and was warmly received by Paao. Lonopele sent a storm to destroy the canoes. Probably he launched his own fleet and made pursuit. Two great fish aided the fugitives. The Aku pushed the boats. The Opelea hindered the storm waves by opposing his great body and breaking their force. Lonopele ordered his magic bird to take up great waves of water and pour them from the sky, overwhelming the fugitives. The canoe-men hurriedly arranged mats covering the boats, and the water was turned into the sea. Thus they escaped.

The days passed. Sometimes showers fell upon the mats arranged like funnels, filling the water calabashes afresh. Sometimes they passed through a school of fish, and caught all they could, drying them for future use. Some died and descended to the "bountiful islands in the world under the waters." Some of the canoes were abandoned. And they sailed on almost hopelessly, still moving northward.

One day Paao said: "I was watching the stars last night and my thought is that some water-god has put his hands under out boats and moved us away from Hawaii."

An astrologer said: "I have heard the pilots

from the burning islands talk about the water-gods and one of them claimed that sometimes a strange god had turned their boats from a straight path."

The action of the ocean currents was supposed to be the malicious work of some strange deity.

That night Paao could not sleep. He studied the stars. He felt a breeze that seemed to him in some way different from the ordinary sea-breezes.

"Do you feel the new wind from the eastern star?" he said softly to his steersmen.

"Aye!" they replied. "We have to hold the steering paddles more firmly."

Paao awakened his prophet and whispered: "Does the new wind have a voice for you?"

The prophet sniffed the air, then stepped upon the high prow and breathed again.

"Aye, the wind has the voice of smoke, perhaps the smoke of the burning-mountain."

"Say nothing about the voice. We will change our course and sail toward the bright star."

During the day the men said, "this is a new wind and it has the storm voice."

The next day came, and then the next. Paao and his prophet alternated between hope and fear. The awful suffering of hunger and thirst was among them. If a mistake had been made there was no possible escape from starvation. In the very early morning of the third day, as Paao was restlessly looking eastward, his wife crept to his side.

"O my Paao," she said, "I am about to die. I have just dreamed of the green-walled paradise. I smelled the sweet Maile blossoms and the leaves of our marriage wreath. I saw the spirits of my sons stand by the cocoanut tree. The vision is from the gods, I must surely die."

"Hush," said Paao quickly, "I too have heard the voice of the Maile born on the winds but I was awake. You shall not die. Call the astrologer, and then listen to his words."

The astrologer came quickly.

"Take breath strong and deep and tell me what the winds say."

"I hear no voice," was the reply.

Paao handed his friend a calabash with a little precious water, bidding him bathe his parched mouth and nostrils.

"Now what do the winds say?"

"Hawaii! Hawaii!! and the strong voice of the Maile blossoms, and the gentle voice of the sugar-cane. I can hear the bread-fruit call 'Come and eat.' The Lau-hala's voice comes over the sea. Awake, awake, oh canoe-men! The fingers of the morning touch the mountains of Hawaii. The morning is raising its hand to beckon us on. O friends of the canoes, awake! Hear the land voices. Hear the wind that has no salt in it. Awake and hear Hawaii."

In a moment shouts and songs of gladness were heard from all the canoes. When hope begins to grow, it ripens rapidly. New life, new strength, pervaded the weakened wanderers. The steersmen unconsciously changed the course of the boats toward the blue haze of land outlined by the dawn.

Thus the day passed. There was no longer any need to husband food. They ate the last morsels. They drained the water from their calabashes. They cheered each other from boat to boat. They toiled hard in rowing, and as the night dropped its shadows around them, they made preparations for landing in this new home.

Bundles of feather robes were unrolled. Native cloth, brilliantly coloured, was taken from its wrappings. Paao robed himself in a high-priest's tabu mantle of black feathers, wearing a white helmet ornamented with black plumes. Around the short masts they placed new mats as sails, inscribed with strange and mysterious emblems. All the people put on their most gorgeous and costly apparel.

Thus, as the new morning dawned, they came to Hawaii. Thus they landed as if their journey had known nothing of starvation and death. Thus they met the wondering natives who hastened along the beach to the spot where the boats must land.

Greetings were given. The language of the newcomers was almost identical in meaning and pronunciation with the native tongue. The priests with new gods were received with offerings. Food and clothing in abundance were given. Land in

Puna, near Hilo, was set apart for their dwelling-place. Paao, aided by the Hawaiians, at once built a temple at Wahaula, which after being twice restored, was destroyed in 1820. From Paao, the high priest's family, highest in priestly rank of all dwelling in the islands, was perpetuated, until Ka-meha-meha's high priest, Hewa-hewa, a lineal descendant of Paao, in 1819, aided in destroying the temples of the gods. With his own hands Hewa-hewa set fire to shrines and idols, overthrowing the system of worship and sacred tabu which Paao had established nearly 700 years before. Some years later Hewa-hewa became a devoted adherent to Christianity.

Some time during the fifth or sixth centuries two Polynesian brothers, sons of Kii, came to the Hawaiian group with a number of followers. They belonged to a high chief family and appeared to have assumed authority without opposition. They divided the islands. Ulu took Maui and Hawaii. Nanaulu settled on Oahu, taking possession of Oahu, Kauai and Molokai.

Kapawa was the last high chief of unblemished blood in the Ulu line on Hawaii.

The Nanaulu line maintained its independence through all the centuries, until it was finally absorbed by the Ka-meha-meha family. The Ulu line in Hawaii was replaced by a Samoan family of high chiefs brought into Hawaii by Paao, in connection with the overthrow of Kapawa.

The high chiefs of "the good old days of Hawaii" had certain prerogatives which were never questioned. They were his by "divine right." He visited the inferior chief of any district at pleasure. He was readily supplied with all the available kapa cloth of the district for clothing and sleeping mats for himself and followers. The hunters of the district were required to search the mountain forests for birds of rare plumage, whose feathers the women were required to weave in mantles and helmets. All the food of the district was subject to his command. He levied upon any canoe attracting his fancy. Food and cloth and canoes were the wealth of the islands. The high chief usually left each district impoverished. There was no complaint against Kapawa on this score, although he had used his "divine right" in the most burdensome manner. The idle, the dissolute, the depraved and the reckless among the sub-chiefs of the various islands flocked to Kapawa and became his "eating companions"—those who received from his bounty their food and clothing. The atrocious lives which such men lived in any community can be imagined. But this was not criminal.

When the Hawaiian legends say "The Ulu line of high chiefs became extinct on account of the crimes of Kapawa," something must be considered besides property, morality or human life. It was not until the sanctity of the temples was attacked that the chiefs decided that even royal blood of many generations might become too impure for a ruling chief.

One day the district chief of Hilo came to the temple, asking to see "the priest of the brother tongue, who worshipped the two round white gods."

When he was brought before Paao he said:

"I speak to you as to a brother. But I must first ask if the priest from afar will make his home by the burning mountain?"

"Aye," said Paao.

"The priest is wise and knows the genealogies of the chiefs, the sons of the gods. He knows the chant of the royal line of Hawaii."

Paao bowed his head.

"The priest understands that our high chief, Kapawa, is descended from Ulu. Is the priest aware that Kapawa is cruel and evil, that he tramples the life out of the land and that he violates the temples and drags out of the city of refuge the man who has safely entered therein? Does the priest know that the high chief is already planning to visit him, to examine his stores and secure whatever new ornaments have been brought from Samoa?"

"I fear no king. I am the voice of the gods. I am the friend of 'Lono, who walks on the sea.' I fear no man," replied Paao, quietly.

"True," said the chief. "Nevertheless the gods aid the man who crosses the channel in a canoe a little more than the man who tries to cross by swimming. We must plan together and hew out our canoe. We want you to consult the gods and tell us their will."

Paao was practical. He knew that by becoming the high priest of the chiefs he would establish his position in Hawaii. He knew the value of advice that comes through mysterious channels.

He went into the temple. After some time he returned and said to the chief:

"The gods answer slowly. They show that you must gather the chiefs upon whom you can depend and have the hard wood prepared for making spears."

"The bird that speaks" flew to Kapawa with the news that the priest from afar was seeking the wisdom of the gods to use against him, and that the chiefs were organising a rebellion.

Several weeks of weary warfare followed.

Kapawa was driven from refuge to refuge. All the district chiefs finally deserted him, and gave adherence to Paao.

The defeated king fled across the channel between the Islands of Hawaii and Maui.

He sought the Maui branch of the Ulu descendants, a discouraged and ruined king.

The legends say that here he died. His body was placed in the royal burial cave, in Iao Valley, back of the village Wailuku. The native custodians of this cave guard its secrets jealously. Probably none of the white residents have seen its mysteries.

Thus the old royal family of Hawaii was over-thrown, and the way prepared to introduce "Pili, the king, from a foreign land."

Paao was afraid that the district chiefs would ask him for a high chief as soon as they should come together. Some of the chiefs had already said, "It may be the will of the gods that the high priest become the high chief also."

But Paao knew the inherent reverence of the Polynesians for blood-royal. He knew his own power. He felt that his position as high priest was unassailable. He wanted no civil entanglements. He had managed through all the campaign, to sur-round himself with mysteries, and had gained un-bounded influence through arousing superstitious fears as well as through warlike deeds.

The Hawaiian legends tell us Pili, a very high chief of Samoa, was persuaded by messengers from Paao to move to the islands of the north.

Pili journeyed with, what the legend called, a "cloud of boats." It was an eleventh century mi-gration of a small nation to a distant home.

Thus was Pili set apart as King of Hawaii.

From Hilo, the eleventh century king went to the beautiful Waipio Valley, taking Paao with him. Later he moved to the Kohala district. Here Paao built the Mookini temple, in a place to which he gave the name it still bears—Lae Upolu, the Cape of Upolu.

Here, in Kohala, from the eleventh century to 1819, the high priests and the chiefs of Hawaii made their home. The priest and the king stand out from the mists of the past, representing two great forces of Hawaiian government—the religious and the civil. Independent of each other, the rights of each were jealously guarded.

Paao gave Pili no chance for choice. While he granted to the king civil authority, he retained absolutely independent control over the minds of the chiefs and the people in religious matters.

Ka-meha-meha, the most noted person of all Hawaiian history, was a descendant in a straight genealogical line from Pili, and Hewa-hewa, the Christian, was the last high priest of the Paao line.

This is the story of the founding of the Ka-meha-meha family. The legends have been shorn of the fabulous element which naturally gathered around them, in order that the true names and customs of the time might be delineated.

One of the most important results was the establishment of an Aha-alii—council of chiefs—or herald's college, which demanded the genealogy and proof of high birth, before admission was granted to the privileges of rank. In meeting this demand genealogies became of great importance. The separation between chiefs and common people became a gulf fixed by custom.

VIII

MOI-KEHA, THE RESTLESS

FOLKLORE is sometimes the outgrowth of a sympathy with nature, resulting in nature myths and sometimes it is an outgrowth of sympathy with history. The imagination loves a truth in nature or in history and weaves around it a web of thoughts of things which might have been.

The story of Moi-keha, the restless, is an historical myth. There are some unquestioned facts and much which was impossible.

Fornander, the omnium-gatherum of Hawaii, thinks Moi-keha lived in the thirteenth century.

The two boys, Moi-keha and Olopana, were born on the island of Oahu.

Their boyhood was like that of other Hawaiian youths of high chief blood. They studied the spear and surf-board exercises. They gambled with hidden stones. They sported with discus and javelin throwing. They raced down green hillsides with their long coasting sleds. They wrestled and fought with their companions and listened to the tales of the sea rovers of the Pacific. They learned the routes to the southern and southeastern islands and heard with fired imaginations the descriptions of Tahiti and Samoa. If the Romans believed that an ocean of thick mist, peopled with all imaginable terrors lay to the north of Europe, we can well accept the fact that strange fascinations and the hope of marvellous adventures in the South Pacific might stir the restless minds of young Hawaiian chiefs.

Moi-keha and Olopana gathered a strong band of brave retainers and, bidding farewell to Oahu, as their ancestors had done before them, sailed toward the South.

For some reason the brothers took with them a young chief of high position, whose ancestor, Pau-makua, had made renowned voyages to far-off lands. The story of Laa, who, in late life, was known as "Laa from Tahiti," must be reserved for later record. Moi-keha, however, seems to have taken this young man under his own especial protection as his foster son.

The company from Kauai stopped at Waipio Valley, on the island of Hawaii, one of the most beautiful and inaccessible valleys of the whole Hawaiian group.

Here Olopana was set apart as ruler of the district.

The days and nights were filled with fishing and feasting, ruling and revelling. Olopana soon found a beautiful young chiefess, who was in full sympathy with his ambitions, whom he took from her home as his life-companion. This woman, Luu-kia, was said to be a descendant of the Nana-ulu line of chiefs, originally coming to Hawaii from Tahiti.

Storms, floods and freshets swept Waipio Valley. The people fled from the scene of disasters. The young chiefs found themselves homeless. Again the love of adventure excited them. They prepared provisions for a voyage of many days. They selected the wisest students of the stars. They plotted their proposed route over the ocean. We are not told that they had any one with them who had already been to Tahiti. It is probable, however, that some of the old prophets and astrologers of their fathers were with the young people as their priestly guardians. They never seemed to doubt their ability to find their way. With their selected companions the two brothers sailed for Tahiti.

Olopana and his wife, Luu-kia, occupied one of the large ocean-going canoes and Moi-keha with Laa sailed in another. Some of the legends say that they went away with a fleet of five large canoes.

The Hawaiian story says that the brothers arrived safely in Tahiti, where Olopana soon became chief of a district known in the legends as "The-open-great-red-Moa." One of the harbours of *Raiatea* of the Tahitian Islands was known as *Ava-Moa,* the Moa Harbour, or "The Sacred Harbour." Fornander justly argues that there is little doubt that this was the place selected by Olopana as his permanent home.

Moi-keha appears to have been the priest of the family, for it is said that he built a temple and called it *Lanikeha* or "the heavenly resting-place."

After a time Moi-keha found that life with his brother was not so pleasant as might be desired, therefore he again prepared for a new voyage, this time returning to his native land. He left Laa with Olopana.

Two of the companions of Moi-keha on this return voyage became famous in the annals of Hawaii. Kama-hua-lele was known through all the ages by his chant in honour of Moi-Keha.

He superintended the building of the strong canoes. He was a *kilokilo*, an astrologer who understood the places of the stars in the heavens and the proper course to steer, guided by the sun by day and the stars by night. He was the poet and seer and *kahu* or guardian of his chief Moi-keha. The expedition was practically subject to his directions.

Laa-mao-mao, who aided Moi-keha as priest of the gods of the winds, later dropped out of the story and moved to the island Molokai, where he was supposed to have made his home near a place known as House of Lono, a well-known hill on that island. Here he took his calabash of winds and became the god of the winds, opening his calabash and letting breezes or storms escape according to the wishes of the one seeking his aid. He controlled the direction in which the winds should travel, by lifting the cover on one side of the calabash. Then the imprisoned winds burst forth and sped away in the desired direction.

It is said that when Moi-keha came back to the Hawaiian Islands he visited all along the island coasts until he came to Kauai. Whenever he landed he seems to have given prominence to one after another of the companions of his long voyage. Places were named after some of them and other places given to others for their future residence.

At last they came to Kauai, the most northerly island of the group. They timed their approach so that the shadows of the night were around them. Then as the light of the morning rose over sea and shore, with his canoes flying the royal banners of a high chief, he drew near.

Kama-hua-lele, standing by the mast which bore the royal colours, sang the chant of Moi-keha. The closing part of the chant is thus translated by Fornander:

> "O, Moikeha, the chief who is to reside.
> My chief will reside on Hawaii.
> Life, life, O buoyant life!
> Live shall the chief and the priest.
> Live shall the seer and the slave,
> Dwell on Hawaii and be at rest,
> And attain to old age on Kauai.
>   O Kauai is the island
>   O Moikeha is the chief."

This chant had been clearly recited wherever Moi-keha had visited any of the islands, and now fell for the first time on the ears of the curious inhabitants of Kauai. The warm welcome was given to Moi-keha and his companions, which was always extended to high chiefs.

King Kalakaua adds a romantic incident to the coming of Moi-keha to Kauai.

Puna, the king, had a daughter who belonged to the fairy tale period of Europe rather than to the free giving and taking in marriage of the Hawaiians. She had many suitors among the young chiefs, but could not decide upon the one highest in her esteem.

Her father at last had decided that the only way to keep her suitors from always living at his cost was to have a contest. This had been agreed upon before the coming of Moi-keha. When Moi-keha saw Hooipo, the daughter of the king, he determined to have her for his wife and planned to enter into the contest.

The king had sent a human hair necklace and whale tooth ornament to be placed on one of the small islands some distance from Kauai. The first chief to secure the necklace should have the king's daughter.

The fine large canoes of the various chiefs with their strong crews of oarsmen were drawn up in line. Moi-keha had only a small canoe prepared which still lay on the shore under the care of one of his comrades from Tahiti.

At the given signal the canoes sped on this journey, but Moi-keha lingered. The young princess had now decided that Moi-keha was the chief she desired, but she could not urge him to go, and still he lingered.

After a time, when the other boats were almost lost to sight, he launched his little canoe, and with his companion, paddled out into the ocean. Then he raised his mast and fastened to it his mat-sail.

Soon the boat leaped through the waters. No paddle was needed save for steering. Laa-mao-mao was in the canoe with him, holding strong winds in his calabash. He let loose these servants just behind the sail and they pushed the canoe forward with incredible rapidity. Long before the other chiefs came in sight of the island Moi-keha had found the necklace and had sailed away to Hooipo.

In time Moi-keha became the king of Kauai.

IX

LAA FROM TAHITI

WHEN history is told by genealogies, rather than by cycles of years, the time-problem is difficult to solve. But in the story of Laa-mai-Kahiki* the stories and genealogies of two widely separated groups of Pacific islands produce a certain degree of apparent accuracy. The Society Islands have the story of Raa who became a ruler and established a line of rulers which has continued to the present day. The genealogy of this Raa family coincides very closely in extent with the number of names given in the Hawaiian genealogies from the time of the visit of Laa from Tahiti to his uncle Moi-keha the Restless and his subsequent return to Tahiti. This places the time of Laa in the thirteenth century.

Moi-keha sailed away from the Hawaiian

* Laa-mai-Kahiki means Laa-from-Kahiki in the Hawaiian language, or Raa-from-Tahiti in the Tahitian dialect. In the Hawaiian stories he was always known as Laa-mai-Kahiki. He was a very high chief from Hawaii absorbed in the royal line of Tahiti. The letter "r" being used for "l" and "t" for "k" explains the slight difference in the names, Laa and Raa-Kahiki and Tahiti. This is simply such a change as is found in dialects everywhere.

Islands with his brother Olopana and his nephew Laa. He returned alone, and won the island Kauai as his kingdom. Olopana and Laa remained in the "wide spreading" valley under the shadow of what the Hawaiians called the mountain Kapa-ahu the Tapa Cloak in far away Tahiti.

The mountains of Tahiti have been built upward from the floors of the ocean until their rugged ravines rise several thousand feet above the surf-washed beach. The centuries have softened the harsh mountain outlines and swept vast masses of debris down into the valleys, until at last tropical luxuriance dominates mountain slope and level plain. Here Laa's youth was spent, and his manhood gained. Here he proved his superiority over the Tahitian chiefs among whom he had found his permanent home. Laa's record is that of a Polynesian viking. He was born on the island Oahu. He went to Hawaii with his uncles and spent a part of his boyhood in the royal valley of Waipio. With these same uncles he sailed the many hundred miles to Tahiti.

It has always been the ambition of Hawaiian chiefs to excel in all athletic sports and warlike exercises. This was a course of training well fitted to make Laa high-spirited, courageous and ever ready to take the leadership among his fellow-chiefs in the new land where he made his home.

Years passed by. Moi-keha was held back

from longed-for sea journeys by the cares of his
kingdom and the restful delights of a prosperous
home. Children whose names became noted in
Hawaiian legends grew to manhood and woman-
hood around him. Kahai, the sea-rover, a
grandson of Moi-keha, is said to have sailed to
Upolu in the Samoan Islands and there found a
new species of breadfruit which he thought might
well be placed by the older Hawaiian breadfruit.
This he brought back with him and planted at
Pearl Harbor.

Kila, the third son of Moi-keha, was made a
messenger to Tahiti by his father. A great long-
ing had taken possession of Moi-keha to see the
foster son whom he had carried away many years
before. Kila was said to be very careful and courageous with a strong desire to emulate the deeds
of his ancestors. The call to the sea was hereditary and with eagerness he grasped the opportunity. The largest double canoes were selected,
their mat sails were made from new and strong
hala leaves and they were equipped for the long
voyage. Fornander says that some of Kila's
brothers went with him. The old astrologer and
sailor, Kama-hua-lele, who had come from Tahiti
with Moi-keha, was selected to be the guardian of
the young chiefs and pilot of the expedition.

Kila sailed from island to island until at last he
left the high mountains of the island Hawaii and

By courtesy Paradise of the Pacific

CHIEFS IN FEATHER CLOAKS AND HELMETS

sailed away to the South. The Kalakaua legends say that Kila bore with him a brilliant royal mantle made from the rare feathers of the mamo, and that Moi-keha had been many months in the manufacture of the mantle, assisted by hundreds of bird hunters and skilled workmen. This was an especial offering to Laa, a reminder of the high esteem in which his foster father still held him, and a proof of the intense desire for him to visit his native land.

The long canoe voyage appears to have been blessed with favouring winds and clear skies. The stars were easily observed and followed until Tahiti was found. It seems to those who now cross the ocean in great ships that such a voyage is almost incredible, but the Hawaiians were vikings and were as intrepid sailors as the Norsemen who were sailing across the Atlantic Ocean about the same time.

At Tahiti they found Laa and his uncle Olopana. Fornander says that one set of legends gives the story of Laa's speedy return to Hawaii with Kila. Another set of legends rehearses the age of Olopana and his desire for Laa to remain with him until his life should end. All the legends agree in stating that Laa returned to the Hawaiian Islands, that he had with him a large retinue when he visited the home of his childhood and that he brought the drum known through all the later years as Ke-eke-eke. It was made by cutting out the pithy heart of a section of a large cocoanut tree, and thinning the shell as far as safety would allow. Then the ends were covered with the skin of a shark. Fornander says that "every independent chief, and every temple where human sacrifices were offered, had their own drum and drummer from Laa-mai-Kahiki's time to the introduction of Christianity."

The great event by which Laa was indelibly impressed upon the legends of Hawaii was his triple marriage with three selected chiefesses of the island Oahu.

The highest chiefs among the Hawaiians were glad to ally themselves with Laa-mai-Kahiki. Not only did the romance of far-away lands and mighty deeds attract attention, but his personal appearance and royal bearing seemed to have conquered all who came near. There was the general feeling that this powerful chief, who would soon return to Raiatea, must leave descendants among the Hawaiians.

Offerings were sent to the temples and the priests were consulted. The most sacred tests were made of the most important auguries known by the priesthood. The decision was announced that Laa must have wives given to him from among the young women of highest rank on Oahu, the home of Laa in his boyhood and still the place where the larger portion of his nearest relatives resided.

The daughters of the chiefs of the districts Kua-loa, Kaalaea and Kaneohe, all on the island Oahu, were selected and married to him in the midst of a great round of feasts and games.

It was always known that Laa would return to Tahiti, and yet many inducements were placed before him to lead him to stay. But he only waited until each of the three chiefesses gave birth to a son, and then sailed away to establish a lasting line of rulers in Tahiti, where, according to Tahitian custom, he was called Raa.

The ancient Hawaiian chants recorded the names of the three sons of Laa thus:

> "O Laa from Tahiti, the chief.
> O Ahukini, son of Laa.
> O Kukona, son of Laa.
> O Lauli, son of Laa, the father.
> The triple canoe of Laa-mai-Kahiki.
> The sacred first-born of Laa,
> Who were born on the same one day."

This gift of three sons—a "triple canoe"—to the Hawaiians is one of the most fully accepted facts of the traditions of long ago. They established families of great prominence and their descendants were proud of this distinction as "children of Laa."

Apparently there was little intercourse later with the southern groups of the islands of the Pacific Ocean. The vikings passed away and their descendants failed to conquer the dangers of the seas. It may be that a prolonged season of volcanic activity discouraged sea roving. It is probable that many sailed away and were never heard of again. History seldom records the long list of failures among men. It has been better to tell of victories.

In October of the year 1527, three Spanish ships were "fitted out" by Cortez. They set sail from Zacatula, Mexico, for the Molucca Islands. One only, under the command of Saavedra, reached its destination. A fierce storm drove the little squadron far north of the ordinary route, and swept two of the ships out of the record of history. Alexander says: "It seems certain that a foreign vessel which was wrecked about this time on the Kona coast of Hawaii must have been one of Saavedra's missing ships." From this ship a white man and woman escaped. After reaching the beach they knelt for a long time in prayer. The Hawaiians, watching them, waited until they rose, and received welcome. The place was at once named "Kulou"—"kneeling." Through all the succeeding years the name kept the story of the wrecked white chiefs before the Hawaiian people. The Hawaiians received their white visitors as honoured guests, and permitted them to marry into noted chief-families. In the Hawaiian legends the man and woman are called brother and sister. The man was named Ku-kana-loa. Their descendants were well known, one of them being a governor of the island of Kauai. These white citizens came to the islands in the reign of Ke-alii-o-ka-loa, who was born about A. D. 1500, and became a king of Hawaii about A. D. 1525.

There seems to be scarcely a trace of the Spanish language or of the Christian religion as prac-

ticed by the Spaniards. The nearest approach to
any permanent influence possibly coming from this
shipwrecked man is the statement made to a chief
by a native prophet long before the islands were
discovered by Captain Cook, that from his prede-
cessors he had learned the prophecy: "A commu-
nication would be made to them from Heaven, the
place of the real God, entirely different from anything they had known and that the tabu of the
country would be subverted."

The Hawaiian traditions have several references
to foreigners coming to the islands. Pau-makau,
of Oahu, was one of the Vikings of the Pacific
during the twelfth century. He is recorded as visiting many foreign lands. He brought priests to
Oahu. Judge Fornander suggests that quite possibly these were Indians from the American coast.
Professor Alexander, in his "History of Hawaii,"
thinks there is scarcely sufficient foundation for
the suggestion. However, Pau-makau and his
journeys are accepted as part of Hawaiian history.

In the thirteenth century "the white chief
with the iron knife" was wrecked on the coast
of the island of Maui, near the village Wai-
luku. Three men and two women were saved.
Wakalana, a chief, took his outrigger canoe
through the surf and rescued them. These persons are supposed to have been Japanese. The
captain of the ship carried a long sword which became renowned throughout the islands as "the

wonderful iron knife." It was a tremendously effective weapon, when matched with wooden daggers and war clubs. King Kalakaua relates the amplified legend and chant in his "Myths and Legends of Hawaii," and in imagination pictures some of the battles fought and trades made for the possession of the iron knife. The Hawaiians came from all parts to see these remarkable strangers. They were astonished to see the women eat the same kinds of food, and from the same dishes as the men. "Nothing was tabu to the strangers." This was entirely new to Hawaiian ideas. Another legend mentions a foreign ship, called Ulupano, and the captain was remembered as Malolano. It is supposed that the ship soon sailed away. Other hints are found of ships having been seen out on the ocean by fishing parties who had gone far from land. These ships were called *moku* [islands], the name used to the present day.

There are undoubted proofs of the discovery of the Hawaiian Islands in 1555 by the Spaniard, Juan Gaetano. This is the first known record of the islands among the civilised nations. There are evident references to this group in the legends of the Polynesians in other Pacific islands.

Gaetano passed through the northern part of the Pacific and discovered large islands which he marked upon a chart as "Los Majos." The great mountains upon these islands did not rise in sharp peaks, but spread out like a high tableland in the clouds, hence he also called the islands "Isles de Mesa," the Mesa Islands or the Table Lands. One of the islands was named "The Unfortunate." Three other smaller islands were called "The Monks."

Le Perouse, the celebrated Frenchman who visited Hawaii in A. D. 1796, says that Gaetano saw these islands "with their naked savages, cocoanuts and other fruits, but no gold or silver." There was nothing attractive, and the wealth-loving Spaniard marked the islands on his chart and never visited them again. So the record lay for many years. This record, kept in Spain's archives, is now accepted as marking the real discovery of the Hawaiian Islands.

Meanwhile, the Hawaiians were as completely ignorant of the rest of the world as if no civilised eyes had ever seen their mountains. They offered each other as human sacrifices; they fought for supremacy. They died at the will of their chiefs. They lived almost as lustfully as the brutes. They had nothing that could be called a home, with an affectionate household gathered inside its walls. They ate, and slept, and died. They entered with zeal into the national sports as well as into the national quarrels. They chanted their genealogies and personal prowess. The art of sailing long distances by the aid of the stars had fallen into disuse. The age of the Western Vikings had passed by. For three or four hundred years no voyagers had found their way to foreign lands. Then some time in the early part of the eighteenth century a king of Oahu involuntarily made a journey which was celebrated as a part of his genealogical chant. The entire "mele," or song, stretches out to about six hundred lines. It is an interesting poem filled with graphic references to people and places, to winds and seas, and to birds and fishes.

In this chant the king of Oahu relates his strange experience on the ocean. Fornander quotes the poem in his "Polynesian Race":

CHANT OF KU-ALII (KU—THE CHIEF)

"O Kahiki, land of the far reaching ocean.
  Within is the land—outside is the sun,
  Indistinct are the sun and the land when approaching.
      Perhaps you have seen it.
      I have seen it.
      I have surely seen Kahiki.

"A land with a strange language is Kahiki.
  The men of Kahiki have ascended
  The backbone of heaven (mountains)
  Up there they trample down,
  They look down on those below.
  Men of our race are not in Kahiki.
  One kind of men is in Kahiki—the white man.
      He is like a god.
      I am like a man,
      A man, indeed.

"Wandering about, the only Hawaiian there.
  Days and nights passing by.
  By morsels was the food.
  Picking the food like a bird.
      Listen, O bird of Victory!
      Hush, with whom was the victory?
          With Ku, indeed."

The chant states that the king was "wandering about," probably driven by the winds far south from the islands. He and his oarsmen were almost starving. The food became "morsels," or only enough for a bird to "pick up." But Ku— the chief—won the victory over the ocean. He went to the "foreign land." He found the white man's home, where the "land was 'within,'" *i. e.,* lying to the east, with the sun "outside," *i. e.,* westward over the waters, most of the day. Perhaps the misty mountains concealed the sun until the forenoon was far spent. He saw "the land of the far-reaching ocean," and returned in safety to Oahu. "With Ku—the chief—indeed was the victory."

Judge Fornander says: "It is probable that some Spanish galleons picked up Ku and his companions, carried them to Acapulco, Mexico, and brought them back on the return voyage."

In 1743, Lord Anson, of the British ship *Centurion,* captured a Spanish ship near the Philippine Islands, and found a chart locating a group of islands in the North Pacific—the same group that Gaetano discovered in 1555. This chart, and the story of Lord Anson's voyage, were almost certainly known by Captain Cook, who made three voyages through the Pacific.

XI

CAPTAIN COOK

IN response to an appeal from the British Admiralty, Captain Cook left England to enter upon his third voyage in July, 1776, with the purpose of restoring some natives of the Society Islands to their home; examining islands of the Pacific for good harbours for future English use; and then to pass along the northwest coast of America to find, if possible, a sea passage from the Pacific Ocean to Hudson's or Baffin's Bay. During the year 1777 he felt his way from island group to island group. He recognised the close relationship in language and features, between inhabitants of many of these island worlds.

On January 18, 1778, he discovered Oahu and later Kauai, of the Hawaiian Islands. He named the group "The Sandwich Islands," in honour of Lord Sandwich, the patron of the expedition.

This name has never been accepted among the Hawaiians. The home name, the name used for centuries, could not be supplanted by an English discoverer. The Hawaiians have always called themselves "Ka poe Hawaii"—"the Hawaiian people."

There are four different sources of information concerning the coming to and death of Captain Cook in the Hawaiian Islands. Captain King wrote the account given in "Cook's Voyages."

Ledyard, an American petty officer on one of Captain Cook's ships, wrote a story published in America.

The surgeon on Captain Cook's boat kept a diary which has recently been published.

The historian must remember that there were thousands of native eye-witnesses whose records cannot be overlooked in securing a true history. The following account is almost entirely from the Hawaiians only:

Captain Cook came to Waimea, Kauai. He was called by the Hawaiians *"O Lono,"* because they thought he was the god Lono, one of the chief gods of the ancient Hawaiians.

The ship was seen coming up from the west and going north. Kauai lay spread out in beauty before Lono, and the first anchor was dropped in the bay of Waimea, in the month of January, 1778. It was night when the ship anchored.

A man by the name of Mapua, and others, were out fishing, with their boats anchored. They saw a great thing coming up, rising high above the surf, fire burning on top of it. They thought it was something evil and hurried to the shore, trembling and frightened by this wonderful apparition. They had fled, leaving all they had used

while fishing.   When they went up from the beach
they told the high chief Kaeo and the other chiefs
about this strange sight.

In the morning they saw the ship standing outside Waimea.   When they saw this marvellous
monster, great wonder came to the people, and they
were astonished and afraid.   Soon a crowd of
people came together, shouting with fear and confused thought until the harbour resounded with
noise.   Each one shouted as he saw the ship with
masts and the many things, such as ropes and sails,
on them.   One said to another, "What is this
thing which has branches?"   Another said, "It is
a forest of trees."   A certain priest, who was also
a chief, said, "This is not an ordinary thing; it is
a *heiau* [temple] of the god Lono, having steps
going up into the clear sky, to the altars on the outside" (*i. e.,* to the yards of the upper masts).

The chiefs sent some men to go out in canoes
and see this wonderful thing.   They went close to
the ship and saw iron on the outside of the ship.
They were very glad when they saw the amount
of iron.   They had known iron before because of
iron in sticks washed up on the land.   Then there
was little, but at this time they saw very much.
They rejoiced and said, "There are many pieces of
pahoa" (meaning iron).   They called all iron *pahoa*
—a tool for cutting, because there was once a
sword among the old people of the Islands.

They went up on the ship and saw "a number

of men with white foreheads, shining eyes, skin wrinkled, square-cornered heads, indistinct words, and fire in their mouths."

A chief and a priest tied the ends of their long malo-like sashes and held them up in their left hands. "They went before *Kapena Kuke* (Captain Cook), bent over, squatted down, and offered prayers, repeating words over and over; then took the hand of Kapena Kuke and knelt down; then rose up free from any tabu."

Captain Cook gave the priest a knife. For this reason he named his daughter *Kua-pahoa,* after this knife. This was the first present of Captain Cook to a Hawaiian.

When they saw the burning of tobacco in the mouth of a man they thought he belonged to the volcano family. When they saw peculiar and large "cocoanuts" (probably melons) lying on the deck, they said, "This is the fruit of a sorceress, or mischief-maker of the ocean, who has been killed." They saw the skin of a bullock hanging in the front part of the ship and said, "Another mischief-making sorceress has been killed. Perhaps these gods have come that all the evil *kupuas* [monsters] might be destroyed."

These messengers returned and told the king and chiefs about the kind of men they had seen, what they were doing, their manner of speech, and the death of some of the monsters of the ocean. "We saw the fruit and the skin hanging on the altar.

There is plenty of iron on that temple and a large amount is lying on the deck."

When the chiefs heard this report they said, "Truly this is the god *Lono* with his temple."

The people thought that by the prayer of the priest all troubles of tabu had been lifted, so they asked the priest if there would be any trouble if they went on this place of the god. The priest assured them that his prayer had been without fault and there would be no death in all that belonged to the gods. There was no interruption of any kind during the prayer.

Hao was another name for "iron" and also hao meant "theft."

A certain war-chief said, "I will go and *hao* that *hao* treasure, for my profession is to *hao*" (steal). The chiefs assented. Then he paddled out to the ship and went on board and took iron and went down. Some one shot him and killed him. His name was Kapu-puu (The Tabu Hill). The canoes returned and reported that the chief had been killed by a *wai-ki* (a rush of smoke like water in a blow-hole).

Some of the chiefs cried out, "Kill this people because they killed Kapu-puu!" The priest heard the cry and replied, "That thought is not right. They have not sinned. We have done wrong because we were greedy after the iron and let Kapu-puu go to steal. I forbade you at first, and established my law that if any one should steal, he shall suffer the loss of his bones. It is only right that we should be pleasant to them. Where are you, O Chiefs and People! This is my word to you!"

That night guns were fired and sky-rockets sent up into the sky, for the sailors were glad to have found such a fine country. The natives called the flash from the guns *"Ka huila"* (lightning) and *"Kane-hikili"* (thunder of the god *Kane*). The natives thought this was war.

Then a high chiefess, Ka-maka-helei, the mother of Kaumu-alii, the last king of Kauai, said: "Not for war is our god, but we will seek the pleasure of the god." So she gave her own daughter as a wife for Lono—Captain Cook. After this there was promiscuous living among the men of the ship and the people of the land, with the result that the vile diseases of the white people were quickly scattered over all the islands.

A boat came to Oahu from Kauai with a chief. The Oahu people asked him, "What kind of a thing was the ship?" The chief said "it was like a *heiau* (temple) with steps going up to the altars, masts standing with branches spread out each side, and a long stick in front like the sharp nose of a swordfish, openings (portholes) in the side and openings behind. The men had white heads with corners, clothes like wrinkled skin, holes in the sides (pockets), sharp-pointed things on their feet, fire in their mouths, and smoke with the fire like a volcano coming from their mouths."

Kalaniopuu, king of Hawaii, was at Koolau, Maui, fighting with the people of Kahekili, king of Maui. Moho, a messenger, told Kalaniopuu and the chiefs the news about this strange ship. They said, "This is Lono from Kahiki."

They asked about the language. Moho, putting his hand in his malo, drew out a piece of a broken calabash and held it out like the foreigners, saying: "A hikapalale, hikapalale, hioluio, oalaki, walawalaki, waiki, poha, aloha kahiki, aloha haehae, aloha ka wahine, aloha ke keiki, aloha ka hale." Of course, this was a jumbled mass of words or sounds with but very little meaning.

The natives relate how, with veneration, they received the white man. They robed Captain Cook with red native cloth and rich feather cloaks. They prostrated themselves before him. They placed him in the most sacred places in their temples. When he despoiled a temple of its woodwork and carried off idols for firewood to use upon his ships, the natives made no protest. They supposed that Lono had a right to his own. But afterward, when death proved that Captain Cook was "a man and no god," the feeling of resentment was exceedingly deep and bitter. This was the standpoint from which the Hawaiians welcomed their discoverers.

On the other hand, when Captain Cook saw the islands in 1778, he was impressed with the friendly spirit of the people, and with their hearty willingness to give aid in any direction. There was also an appearance of manliness and dignity about the high chiefs. There was such respect and ready service on the part of the people—there were such prostrations before the kings of the various islands that Captain Cook accepted the "worship" offered him as the proper respect due to the representative of Great Britain. He was glad to receive a welcome that freed him from much anxiety. He was thankful that the chiefs accepted his superiority. He could easily procure the supplies needed for his ships. He could prosecute his investigations concerning harbours and resources without danger to himself or to his men.

After securing such supplies as he needed, in February, 1778, he sailed for North America. Here he spent the summer and fall, exploring the coast from San Francisco to Alaska. He consulted the Russians who were fur-hunting in this region. He became satisfied that there was no northwest channel across North America, to either Hudson's or Baffin's Bay. He made a chart of the coast. The winter came on suddenly and severely. He fled to the "Sandwich Islands," and in November, 1778, sighted the island of Maui, or, as Captain Cook phonetically spelled it, "Mowee." Soon he discovered the large island Hawaii, or "Owhyhee." He was surprised to see the summits of the mountains covered with snow. As he drew near the channel between Maui and Hawaii, Ka-meha-meha with several of his friends went on board one of the ships and passed the night. He was at that time forty-three years of age.

Then for eleven days Captain Cook sailed in the channel between Maui and Hawaii. On the second day of December he anchored near Kohala, the northern point of the island Hawaii.

Captain Cook purchased pigs for a piece of iron or barrel hoop, to make axes or knives or fish-hooks. A pig one fathom long would get a piece of iron. A longer pig would get a knife for a chief. If a common man received anything, the chief would take it. If it was concealed and discovered the man was killed.

They brought offerings—pigs, taro, sweet potatoes, bananas, chickens, and all such things as pleased Captain Cook.

Lono went to the western bay Ke-ala-ke-kua and the priest took him into the temple, thinking he was their god. There they gave him a place upon the platform with the images of the gods—the place where sacrifices were laid. The priest stepped back after putting on Captain Cook the *oloa* (the small white tapa thrown over the god while prayer was being recited) and the red cloak *haena,* as was the custom with the gods. Then he offered prayer thus:

"O Lono! your different bodies in the heavens, long cloud, short cloud, bending cloud, spread-out cloud in the sky, from Uliuli, from Melemele, from

Kahiki, from Ulunui, from Haehae, from Ana-okuululu, from Hakalanai, from the land opened up by Lono in the lower sky, in the upper sky, in the shaking bottom of the ocean, the lower land, the land without hills.

"O Ku! O Lono! O Kane! O Kanaloa! the gods from above and from beneath, gods from most distant places! Here are the sacrifices, the offerings, the living things from the chief, from the family, hanging on the shining cloud and the floating land! *Amama* (amen); *ma noa*" (the tabu is lifted).

Several weeks passed by. Trivial troubles arose. The natives learned to steal some things from the supposed "heavenly" visitors. The harmony between the sailors and the Hawaiians was disturbed.

In February, 1779, Lono went on his ship and sailed as far as Kawaihae. He saw that one of his masts was rotten, so he went back to make repairs, and anchored again at Ke-ala-ke-kua. When the natives saw the ships returning they went out again, but not as before. They had changed their view, saying: "These are not gods; they are only men." Some, however, persisted in believing that these were gods. Some of the men said, "They cry out if they are hurt, like any man." Some of them thought they would test Lono, so went up on the ship and took iron. The sailors saw them and shot at them. Then the natives began to fight. The sailors grabbed the canoe of the chief Polea, an *aikane* (close friend) of the king.

He opposed their taking his boat and pushed them off. One of them ran up with a club and struck Polea and knocked him down. The natives saw this and leaped upon the sailors. Polea rose up and stopped the fighting. Because he was afraid Lono would kill him he stopped the quarrel.

After this he no longer believed that Lono was a god. He was angry, and thought he would secretly take one of the ship's boats, break it all to pieces for the iron in it, and also because he wanted revenge for the blow which knocked him down. This theft of a boat was the cause of the quarrel with, and death of, Captain Cook.

Captain Cook and his people woke up in the morning and saw that his boat was gone. They were troubled, and Captain Cook went to ask the king about the boat. The king said, "I do not know anything about it. Perhaps some native has stolen it and taken it to some other place." Captain Cook returned to the ship and consulted with his officers. They decided they had better get the king, take him on the ship, and hold him until the boat should be returned, and then set him free. Officers and men took guns and swords and prepared to go ashore and capture the king.

Captain Cook tried to persuade the king to go to the ship with him. The king was held back by his chiefs. They were suspicious, but the king could not readily give up his confidence.

Meanwhile, a chief living across the bay saw Captain Cook going ashore. He and another chief launched a double canoe and sailed quickly across.

Sailors saw these men in red cloaks, fired upon them from the ships and killed one of them. The other hurried his boatmen and escaped to the king's house. Captain Cook had issued an order forbidding canoes to come near the ships. When the chief saw the king by the side of Captain Cook he cried out: "O Kalani! O the sea is not right—Kalimu has been killed! Return to the house!" He told how the sailors had fired upon his friend and himself.

Kalola, wife of Kalaniopuu, heard the death-word, and that the chief had been killed by the gun of the foreigners, so she ran out of the woman's house, put her hand on the king's shoulder and said, "O Kalani, let us go back."

The king turned, thinking he would go back, but Captain Cook seized his hands. A chief thrust his spear between them, and the king and some of his chiefs went back to the house.

Then the battle commenced. When Lono (Captain Cook) saw the spear pushed between the king and himself he caught his sword and struck that chief on the head, but the sword slipped and cut the cheek. Then that chief struck Lono with his spear and knocked him down on the lava beach.

Lono cried out because of the hurt. The chief thought, "This is a man, and not a god, and there is no wrong." So he killed Lono (Captain Cook). Four other foreigners also were killed. Many daggers and spears were used in killing Captain Cook.

When the officers and men saw that Captain Cook and some others had been killed, they ran down, got on the boat, fired guns and killed many of the natives. Some natives skilled in the use of sling-stones threw stones against the boat. When the sailors saw that Captain Cook was dead, they fired guns from the ship. The natives held up mats as shields, but found they were no protection against the bullets.

The king offered the body of Captain Cook as a sacrifice. This sacrifice meant that the body was placed on an altar with prayers as a gift to the gods because the chief and his kingdom had been saved by the gods. When the ceremonies of the sacrifice were over, they cleaned off the flesh from the bones of Lono and preserved them. A priest kindly returned a part of the body to the foreigners to be taken on their ship. Some of the bones were kept by the priests and worshipped.

Eight days after the death of Lono at Ka-awa-loa the natives again met those who remained on the ship.

Monday, February 23, 1779, the ship went to Kauai. On the 29th of that month they secured water and purchased food. Because they wanted the yams of Niihau, they sailed over to that island and purchased yams, sweet potatoes, and pigs, and on March 15th sailed out into the mist of the ocean and were completely lost to sight.

This is the end of Captain Cook's voyage along the coasts of these islands.

XII

THE IVORY OF OAHU

KING KAHAHANA, ABOUT 1773

THE story of the ivory of Oahu is a tale of treachery and triumph on the part of Kahekili, King of Maui, and of defeat and death for Kahahana, the last independent king of Oahu.

Kahahana was the son of Elani, chief of Ewa, one of the most powerful among the high chiefs of Oahu. While still a child, he was sent to Maui to pass the years of his young manhood in close contact with one of the most noted courts among the different island kings—the court of his relative, Kahekili.

After many years had gone by the Oahu chiefs deposed their king and drove him away to the island of Kauai. Then they met in a great council to select a new king from the high chief families. After careful consideration, it was decided that Kahahana was the most available of all who could be accepted for their future ruler, and an embassy was sent to Maui to recall him and inform him

114

of the exalted position for which he had been chosen by his fellow-chiefs of Oahu.

The Maui king was wise in his own generation and determined to make all the use possible of this selection.   Therefore, he objected to the young chief's acceptance of the place of ruler of the neighbouring island.   When this objection had been overruled by the high chiefess, who had been sent from Oahu to bring back the young king, Kahekili again delayed proceedings by refusing to permit the young wife to go with him.   Then there came another season of councils and consultations. It was easy for the King of Maui to control the line of thought as advanced by his chiefs.   It seems that they argued that it was best for the wife to go if a suitable return should be made in some way by the new King of Oahu.   Then again it was conceded on all sides that Kahahana was very deeply in debt to his relative for the protection afforded him and the careful and royal attention bestowed upon him in the court of Maui.

Kahekili and his chiefs were pronounced worshippers of the various Hawaiian gods, therefore they argued that they should receive a place on the northeastern shores of Oahu where a noted heiau or temple was located.   The cession of the Kua-loa lands, with this temple, would be a very satisfactory partial recompense.   The young king thought that this was a small part of his kingdom and would scarcely be missed, hence he readily promised to grant the Kua-loa district to his friend.

There were certain gifts of the sea which were very highly prized by all the chiefs of the Hawaiian Islands. Among these, whalebone and the very scarce whale's teeth were most prominent. These were "the ivory" of the Islands. The whalebone and the teeth were called *palaoa*. The "ivory" was usually made into a "hooked ornament" with a large hole almost in the middle, through which was passed a large number of strings of human hairs, thus forming a necklace unique and costly. Small portions of the ivory were pierced and fashioned into beads. These were strung together and also used as necklaces. It was a burial custom to place the *palaoa* in the burial cave in which the bones of any dead chief might be secreted.

Kahekili and his ready followers argued that as a slight return for the royal favour which had been shown to Kahahana in caring for him at court and in permitting his wife to go with him, he could very readily covenant to bestow upon Kahekili all the ivory which might be found on the shores of Oahu. Probably this matter was not presented as the payment of tribute, but as a recognition of benefits received, and Kahahana again readily promised the ivory—the gift of the seas.

This was as far as Kahekili dared to go in his demands. Apparently the two kings then discussed the continuance of the friendly relations which had bound them together so many years, and

entered into some kind of an alliance by which
Kahekili might receive assistance in his wars with
the chiefs of the large island of Hawaii.   Two, or
perhaps three, years after this consultation, Kahahana sent heavy reinforcements from Oahu to
Maui, which aided Kahekili in the complete annihilation of the Alapa Regiment, about eight hundred chiefs, from Hawaii, in the noted "Battle of
the Sand-Hills," near Wailuku.

Soon the morning came for sailing to Oahu.
Kahahana, his wife, and the high chiefess who had
come from Oahu to bring the news of his election,
and a large retinue of retainers left Maui in regal
state, while the good-bye "aloha" rang out over
the waters from crowds of friends.

When the Oahu priests in the heiaus on the
slopes of Leahi or Diamond Head saw the fleet
of canoes coming from Maui, swift runners were
despatched to all the high chiefs of the island that
they might assemble at Waikiki and give welcome
to their new king.   It is not difficult to imagine the
barbaric splendour of the royal canoes and their oc-
cupants as they crossed the outer coral reefs and
drew near to the white sands of the most famous
beach in Hawaiian history.   The canoes were
fitted with triangular sails made from the leaves
of the hala tree, while brilliant pennants floated
from every mast head.   The king and high chiefs
wore the feather cloaks and helmets betokening
their rank.   From these the sunlight flashed in gold

and crimson fire. The retainers wrapped their garments of richly coloured tapa around them, while the boatmen, whose bronzed bodies glistened with freshly applied oil, formed a pleasing background to the gaudy display of those highest in rank. Thus Kahahana came to his own.

The Oahu chiefs made a display no less gorgeous along the sands of Waikiki, as they received their king. Nights were spent in revelry and days in feasting until the ceremonies of installation were completed.

At last Kahahana called the high chiefs and those belonging to the highest priesthood together for consultation concerning the affairs of the kingdom.

At this time he broached the agreement he had entered into with Kahekili concerning the ivory of Oahu and the temple lands of Kualoa.

Kahahana was an elected, rather than a hereditary, king of Oahu. Therefore, when, in 1773, he came from Maui to take the reins of government in his hands, it was very important for him to keep the friendship of the high chiefs who had given him the position. He could not assume any self-sufficient aspect and not care whether the other chiefs were well pleased or not. His power to fulfil his agreement depended upon the willingness of the council of high chiefs to ratify what he had promised.

Kahahana gave in full his reasons for agreeing

to the demands. He spoke of the experience gained in the wars between the kings of Maui and Hawaii, and stated that the bestowal of the ivory and the temple lands upon Kahekili might readily be granted as an honourable return from the chiefs of Oahu for the training given to their young king.

A number of chiefs at once yielded to this argument. It was a strong appeal to their honour. They were willing to pay for what they received. But other chiefs were doubtful of the expediency of this action. They desired to please their king and do all that honour required. Yet the wisdom of doing what was asked was not clear. Moreover, Kahahana was not trained to become a king. He had been kept at the court of Maui because he was a relative of the king. Perhaps the king of Maui was asking more than he ought.

Then arose Ka-o-pulu-pulu, the high priest of Oahu, one of the most far-seeing and statesmanlike men in all the islands. He understood the Maui king and his ambitious designs for the conquest of the islands Molokai and Oahu.

Ka-o-pulu-pulu carefully pointed out the fact that there was a great deal to the demands of Kahekili which did not appear on the surface. The surrender of the temple and the ivory was practically accepting Kahekili as sovereign. It was the same as yielding the independence of Oahu. Kualoa with the temple and the lands surrounding it was, in reality, one of the most sacred places in the islands. Here were kept the two war drums sacred from ancient times. The high priest argued that the chiefs could not afford to give these war drums to Kahekili because the favour and protection of the war gods belonged to the king who could call them by the beating of the drums. Moreover, their anger would be against those who had lightly given away the drum-voices.

Then again the chiefs must remember that the consecrated hill of Ka-ua-kahi would go as a part of the temple lands. This would give to Kahekili a basis for invasion, a powerful influence over the gods of Oahu, and would make it still more difficult for the Oahuans to maintain this independence.

The high priest reminded the chiefs also concerning the ivory of Oahu, that this, too, was a proof of the favour of the gods. This time it meant the gods of the sea. To surrender the ivory would turn away the favour of the gods whose assistance was prayed for in all things connected with the great waters. They must not give to Kahekili the gods of both land and sea.

Again Ka-o-pulu-pulu, the high priest, argued that if Kahahana, this new king, had come with warriors and subdued Oahu, the chiefs of Oahu could have nothing to say concerning the disposition of anything belonging to the island. The conqueror could do as he wished with the people or the land. Inasmuch as the chiefs had called Kahahana to the throne, however, "it would be wrong

for him to cede to another the national emblems
of sovereignty and independence."

This rather full argument from the lips of the
high priest shows the exceedingly strong hold
which the tabus and worship of the gods had upon
the most enlightened and upright men of the days
immediately preceding the discovery of the islands
by Captain Cook.   The chiefs had deeply rooted
principles of loyalty and honour toward each other,
and yet the reign of the gods was supreme even
while accompanied by a host of burdens such as
continual human sacrifices and tabus extremely
hard to bear.

Kahahana and the chiefs of Oahu readily accepted the views of the high priest and decided
that they could not accede to the demands of Kahekili.   One thing, however, remained which they
could do for the Maui king, which would abun-
dantly repay him for all the aid he had ever given
to this young king.   They would offer fleets of
canoes filled with warriors to aid him in his battles
with the king of Hawaii.   In this way friendly
relations and a state of peace would be maintained
between the islands of Oahu and Maui.

Kahekili was greatly disappointed by his failure
to secure the ivory, the gift of the gods, and the
sacred lands with the all-powerful war drums, but
he covered his chagrin as best he could by accepting the offer of warriors, for his spies assured him
that his powerful brother-in-law, the king of Ha-

waii, was preparing an immense army with which
to conquer the whole of Maui. He heard of the
organisation of the two powerful bodies of young
chiefs known in Hawaiian history as "the regiments called *Alapa* and *Pii-pii*." The Alapa regiment alone numbered about eight hundred of the
finest and bravest chiefs of the island of Hawaii.

He felt his inability to meet his Hawaiian enemies alone, therefore he called for aid from Oahu.
Then came the "Battle of the Sand-Hills" below
Wailuku and the defeat of the forces of the king
of Hawaii. It was a dearly purchased victory
which he never could have won without the aid
of the Oahu warriors, and yet he was not profuse
in thanks for the assistance given. The failure to
win the desired grant rankled in his heart and he
still nourished the purpose of securing a foothold
on the island of Oahu. The year after the Battle
of the Sand-Hills, Kahekili found an opportunity
for making his next move.

Kahahana went from Oahu to Molokai to con-
secrate a temple. Oahu had maintained sovereignty over Molokai for some time, therefore the
dedication of a heiau of any importance was in
the hands of the king as the person of highest and
most sacred rank. On Molokai there was also a
large taro patch. This needed attention, and some
time was to be devoted to the oversight of the repairs called for.

Kahekili and his advisers thought this was an

excellent opportunity to renew influence over Kahahana.   The two kings met on Molokai and spent
days in royal entertainments.

At the advice of his high priest, the Maui king
craftily set to work to undermine Kahahana's faith
in the Oahu priesthood.   While the kings visited
and feasted together, Kahekili, from time to time,
introduced remarks concerning the way he was
treated in the matter of the ivory of Oahu.   At
one time, apparently as an offset to the sacred lands
which he did not get, he asked for the large and
fertile tract of land on Molokai known as the lands
of Halawa.   This Kahahana readily gave to him
as land that had been conquered and won from
its inhabitants, concerning which there would be
small dispute.

Then Kahekili insinuated that the high priest
of Oahu, in refusing the grant of the ivory and
the sacred lands, had been very insincere.   He
told Kahahana that the prophet, while pretending
to be friendly to Oahu, had at the same time offered the entire government of Oahu to himself.
Thus he began the distrust which was to lead Kahahana to ultimately destroy this wise and loyal
high priest.   In the various conversations he tried
to impress the Oahu king with the belief that the
prophet was really a traitor instead of a friend.
The king's utter lack of principle and his knowledge of the character of the young king are shown
in the way in which he made Kahahana believe in

his personal friendship.   He took pains, in his wily and apparently open-hearted way, to let it be known that the only reason why he had not become the king of Oahu as well as of Maui was because of his great personal love for his young friend.   He would not stand in the way of one in whom he felt so much interest.   But this personal kindness must not blind the eyes of the young king to the fact that his high priest was practically a traitor.

The young king returned to Oahu with great faith in his enemy and a likewise great unbelief in his friends.   He began a course of action inspired by his Maui advisers which was thoroughly overbearing and capricious and finally created dissension throughout his kingdom.

XIII

THE ALAPA REGIMENT

1776

KA-LANI-OPUU was the Moi, or king, of Hawaii, at whose feet Captain Cook was slain in 1779. He had been the ruling chief since 1754. He was a restless warrior and signalised his reign by bloody battles with the chiefs of the neighbouring island of Maui. The decimation of the Hawaiian race began in these inter-island wars before the coming of the white race.

About 1760 Kalaniopuu attacked the southern coast of Maui and captured the famous fort of Kau-wiki.

For fifteen years the Maui chiefs were not able to recapture it. During these years Kalaniopuu had frequently gathered his best company of warriors and attacked the Maui seacoast. From each invasion he had returned laden with captives and spoil. At last, in 1775, the king was the victim of his own ambition. His supreme desire was to rule two islands instead of one, and he was willing to fight for it.

He carried the war close to the home of Ka-hekili, king of Maui. A battle was fought. There was a great destruction of life and property. This raid received the name "Kalae-ho-hoa"—"pounded on the forehead"—because, as the records say, "The captives were unmercifully beaten on their heads with war clubs." For a time victory was with the invaders; the Maui forces were not prepared for the onset, but warriors were hastily assembled from all parts of the island.

There was a bloody hand-to-hand struggle, in which thrusting with spears and striking with clubs meant almost certain death to those who were not able to get in the first blow.

It was a terrible defeat for Hawaii. The old king had been taken to the coast and placed in his royal double canoe ready to escape if his army could not win the day.

One of the most noted and daring warriors of the time, Ke-ku-hau-pio, held his place against the Maui men while his comrades were driven back. Several antagonists crowded around him. When one fell another took his place. Heavy blows from war clubs and spears beat down the weapons of the stalwart warrior and rained blows upon his head and body. Once and again he swept back the circle of his enemies. But they clung to him. They wearied and wounded him until he began to stagger under the blows against which he furnished imperfect guard. His strength was gone, and hands were outstretched to seize him and carry him as a living sacrifice to the nearest heiau.

Suddenly a giant Hawaiian with a very long and heavy war club scattered the group around the fainting warrior.

As he beat down the Maui warriors his cry rang out: "E kokua! E kokua!"—"To the rescue! To the rescue!"

He gave the old chief a moment's rest while he kept the surrounding crowd at bay; then he dashed against the wall of warriors and broke it down. Turning, he caught the old chief and aided him in hurried retreat, while his terrible war club played with lightning strokes against his foes. The young giant screamed with joy when he struck to earth enemy after enemy. With the insane inspiration of battle he made charge upon charge, as he pushed the confused mass of chiefs and people into an impetuous flight. Then he hastened back to his friend and aided him still further in the retreat.

"It is Ka-meha-meha the sacred," the Maui warriors cried; "the gods are in him. Kaili, the war god, strikes through his arms. We cannot fight against the gods."

So they made way for the whirlwind warrior as he helped his friend to the sea. In a few moments they were in a waiting canoe making their escape to Hawaii.

Ka-meha-meha came from this battle an idolised chief. He fulfilled Carlyle's definition of "King"—"König," "the man who can"—the man who, after the battle, would be "lifted upon his comrades' shields and hailed as hero." From that time the young giant was a recognised leader. His position was substantially the same as that of the king's own sons.

This was a sore defeat for the king of Hawaii. He was humiliated and angry. His self-love and ambition were sorely stricken, but he did not pour out his wrath upon his followers. He cheered them and encouraged them to prepare for new endeavours.

He called upon the high chiefs of the various districts of his island for a more thorough preparation of men and war supplies, that with a new and larger army he might make complete subjugation of Maui.

This was in 1775, at the same time that in America the "Boston tea party" and Battle of Bunker's Hill were being followed by the struggle for freedom on the part of England's colonies. In England, King George was calling upon Parliament for advice and funds wherewith to subdue the blood brothers in America. Both King George and King Kalaniopuu were equally obstinate in the determination to rule the lands across the waters.

The chiefs devoted all the energies of their districts to the preparation for the new war.

The warriors went up into the mountains to find the Kauila—the spear tree—that they might cut down and dry the wood for spears and war clubs and daggers.

The lava ledges were searched for the hardest pa-hoe-hoe—the fine-grained, compact lava, well fitted for tools with which to hew out and smooth the many new canoes needed. The stone age is not so very far away from to-day—in some parts of the world. The forests were searched for the best trees from which canoes could be made. The sound of stone axes and adzes rang throughout the land. Hundreds of workmen hewed and scraped and other hundreds polished, until at last a large fleet of canoes and a vast quantity of weapons were prepared.

The fishermen made new offerings to their gods. Large quantities of fish were caught and dried for the commissary department of the new army.

The cloth-makers sought eagerly for the bark of the woke—the paper mulberry tree. They made offerings to their gods, Hia and Lauhuki, of bark and leaves, with the prayer that the bark might be easily manufactured into the finest cloth. Then they pounded the bark into sheets which they stained with vegetable and mineral dyes. Sometimes they made this paper-cloth into waterproof cloaks and sheets by soaking it in cocoanut or ku-kui nut oil.

Every taro field was carefully cultivated, and

prayers offered and sacrifices made to the hideous images of gods placed at some corner of each field to watch over the growing plants. A large amount of taro must be ready to be pounded into poi the next season for the warriors' poi-bowls.

The large number of young chiefs throughout the island was organised into three bands. The young men of royal blood, the king's sons and their cousins, were set apart as the bodyguard of the old king. They were the Keawe, or "the bearers." They were the supporters of the king in whatever move he might make. They were personally responsible for his safety.

The chiefs who were the boon companions of the royal family, who had the privilege of eating around the royal poi-bowls, were separated into two regiments: the Alapa—"the slender"—and Piipii—"the furious."

The Alapa chiefs were the flower of Hawaiian nobility next to the highest chiefs. Eight hundred warriors were in its ranks. They were of almost equal stature, averaging nearly six feet in height. Their spears were of equal length. The bird-hunters of each chief had scoured the forests for the rich crimson feathers of the iiwi, which were woven into glistening war capes. The regimental uniform—light bamboo helmets, feather-coated and crested with brilliant plumes, added to the majestic appearance of these stalwart chiefs.

Many were the chants and stories about the

prowess of the individuals belonging to this noble band. They were all members of the Aha-alii, or "Company of Chiefs." Their genealogies would give them a welcome and a position in any court on any island.

Allegiance could be transferred from one king to another, or from island to island, without loss of rank. Once a chief, always a chief. There could be no system of degradation from the station conferred by birth.

Allegiance was usually given for family reasons. The blood relatives were loyal even unto death to the king of their own blood. Sometimes for personal reasons, such as intermarriage or friendship, a chief would be led to espouse the cause of a new king. Sometimes captives were given the choice between allegiance or death as a human sacrifice before the gods. If they accepted the new service, they were at once treated like friends and property and marriage secured for them. Insult or injury at the hands of a superior chief was always considered good grounds for a transfer of allegiance.

Chiefs were never made slaves, kauwa hooluki— "wearied servants." The common people were in a state of serfdom akin to European feudalism. Life and property and family were absolutely at the will of the high chief, but the servant could leave everything and seek another master.

In time of war a captured chief, unless claimed as a "blood brother" by a friend in the ranks of the enemy, or accepted by the new king, was sentenced to the heiau, or temple, as a human sacrifice. Each chief of the "Aha-alii" had the right to wear the beautiful feather lei, or wreath, and the feather cape, and the niho palaoa, or ivory hook, suspended from a heavy necklace of human hair. He had the right to sail a canoe stained red, from the mast of which floated a pennant over a red sail.

The bond of brotherhood among chiefs was a matter of individual concern. "Two young men adopted each other as brothers. They were bound to support each other in weal or woe. If they found themselves in opposing ranks, and one was taken prisoner, his friend was bound to obtain his freedom, and there is no record in all the legends and traditions that this singular friendship ever made default." The highest chiefs were called alii-tabu—the tabu chiefs. They were sacred in the eyes of the people, who prostrated themselves with faces in the dust when the high chief came near them. "It was said that certain chiefs were so tabu that they did not show themselves abroad by day."

Alexander says: "It was death for a common man to remain standing at the mention of the king's name."

While this army was being recruited, great preparations were made for the purchase of the favour of the gods. Temples were repaired and the gods reclothed. This was a peculiar ceremony. New kapa, or paper-cloth garments, were made and consecrated to the god with prayer and sacrifices. This cloth for the gods was made from the finest bark of the mulberry tree. It was beautifully coloured and brought to the idol. Another series of prayers and offerings—and frequently a human victim—then the ornamented kapa was wrapped around the image as a war cloak.

Such preparations, on so large a scale, could not be concealed from Kahekili, king of Maui. He also gathered warriors and weapons as far as possible from his subjects. But he felt his weakness and sent an embassy to Oahu. He must have a large body of reinforcements and the only available army must come from Oahu. He knew of only one priest in the island group who refused absolutely to acknowledge the superiority of Holoae, the high priest of Hawaii. Therefore, he had requested the king of Oahu to send the high priest Ka-leo-puu-puu to combat the supernatural powers of the high priest of Hawaii. Both of these high priests were of the highest rank. Priestly prestige and power depended upon genealogy. Each of these priests could look back through a straight line of ancestors, to the days of the Vikings of the Pacific and the sea voyages of the eleventh century.

Holoae was a direct descendant of Paao, the eleventh century priest coming from Upolu, Samoa, to Hawaii. His prerogatives in Hawaii and Maui were unquestioned.

Ka-leo-puu-puu was able to prove beyond question that the mantle of priesthood had never passed out of the family since the days of Pau-makua of the eleventh century. There was strong rivalry between the two priestly lines. Kahekili of Maui desired to bring the two priestly powers into conflict with each other. This was the real beginning of the new war.

New temples were built and old temples repaired by both kings, and all were filled with gods and priests and sacrifices. Prayers and incantations innumerable were used by both parties. Many human sacrifices were laid upon the altars.

At last the Maui priest informed his king that he was assured by the gods of final victory. "The warriors of Hawaii should come like fish into a bay and should be caught in a net." From this suggestion came the plan of battle afterward carried out.

The new year dawned—the year known in the civilised world as 1776. It was the year of the Declaration of Independence in America. It was the year of increased British effort and many reverses on the part of the colonies. It was in this year that King George's dark-skinned brother in ambition, Ka-lani-opuu, set sail with "a cloud of boats." Hundreds of canoes crossed the channel between the two islands and then coasted western Maui.

They landed wherever any little valley on the

LANDING OF WARRIORS

rugged slope of Mt. Hale-a-ka-la—"House of the sun"—afforded soil sufficient to give life or foothold. They destroyed the villages and drove the terrified defenceless people up the lava cliffs to mountain hiding-places.

Early one morning a part of the king's army landed at Maalaea Bay, near the spot where they had been defeated. The chiefs looked over the sandy isthmus lying between the two great Maui mountains—Mt. Hale-a-ka-la and Mt. Iao. On the other side of some sand hills in this isthmus lay Wai-luku, the home of the Maui king. The cry arose: "On to Wai-luku! On to Wai-luku!" No strong force had offered opposition so far in the invasion. It seemed fair to presume that they had completely surprised the Maui warriors.

Through the Wai-luku lands dashes a swiftly flowing stream of clear, cold water, breaking through the foothills of Mt. Iao. The banks of this stream had already been the scene of many a bloody battle, hence the name Wai-luku—"Water of destruction."

It was nearly ten miles away—but that would be only a short morning's race for the hardy chiefs.

The Alapa warriors shouted, "Let us drink of the waters of Wai-luku this day!" The king, surrounded by his bodyguard of royal chiefs, watched the splendid array of warriors as they hastened to surprise the Maui warriors. The king's prophet chanted as they passed him:

"Roll on, roll on, waves of Hawaii!
You are the surf waves.
The war god rides on the surf
To land on the banks of Wai-luku."

Over the long desert isthmus sped the stalwart chiefs on up the divide between the two great mountains, until they saw the valley of the Wai-luku and the ocean waters of the eastern coast. On sped the eight hundred bronzed and sinewy athletes. It was to them an easy race for victory. Below Wai-luku lies a sandy tract through which the winds swept with power. It has long been a tangled group of large rounded sand hills. As they entered this rough region the first serious show of force met the exultant Hawaiians. There was obstinate resistance, but the onset of the Hawaiian chiefs was irresistible. They literally trampled the warriors of Maui beneath their feet. On into the sand hills they rushed, chanting their song of victory. Suddenly their Maui foe disappeared, and in front and rear and on every side rose up hundreds of warriors from Oahu—strangers to the Alapa chiefs.

The scouts of Maui had faithfully reported the movements of Ka-lani-opuu and the coming of the Alapa high chiefs, giving the Maui king time to select and place his allies from Oahu. The wily king had made thorough preparation to catch his enemies "in a net." The ambuscade was not ordinarily a part of Hawaiian warfare. In battle, dependence was placed upon the strong arm rather than in cunning wit. Often the beginning of a battle would be delayed by a series of single conflicts between challenging chiefs, as in the days of European knight-errantry. Banners were seldom carried. Some giant chief with marked helmet towered above his fellows and was the centre around which his followers could gather. Sometimes war gods—images of hideous and distorted features—were carried by priests and thrust into the faces of opponents.

This battle of the Alapa regiment was unlike the ordinary contests. The brave warriors massed their strength and expected to override all opposition.

But when they were drawn into conflict in the sand hills their ranks were broken. They were forced to pass around the obstacles or climb over them.

From every wind-raised hill the Oahu men hurled heavy stones upon the plumed helmets beneath them, and thrust long spears into those who stormed the hillsides.

Still up the loose sand the Alapa warriors struggled, putting to death every foe, as they took possession of one hill after another, while their comrades forced the Oahu warriors back through the winding sand valleys.

The conflict continued hour after hour. The blazing tropical sun filled the struggling warriors with raging thirst, and the waters of the Wai-luku were still nearly a mile away.

Then the struggle toward the stream was checked. The Oahu warriors were continually reinforced by fresh, unwearied men. The broken ranks of the Alapa regiment were met by a constantly increasing host of enemies. Soon the larger bodies were separated into small bands, each one hopelessly surrounded by picked warriors.

Broken helmets and tattered feather cloaks lay crushed and trampled into the sand. Fragments of broken spears, javelins and war clubs lay in splinters under the feet. Naked and bleeding the chiefs raised broken arms to ward off descending blows. They died bravely, avenging themselves to the utmost in their death.

Only one of the large regiment was captured alive. Hundreds of bodies of his companions marked the progress of the fight. This last warrior, Ke-awe-hano—"the silent supporter"—noted for his valour, fought to the last and then was beaten down and captured.

"To the chief! To the chief!" was the cry of the Oahu warriors. The wounded man was carried at once to the camp of the king. They decided that he should be sacrificed to the gods, but his wounds were severe and he died before they could carry him to the temple.

Two other valiant chiefs side by side fought their way through their enemies and escaped. They evidently left before the regiment had been annihilated, for they were unnoticed until they had gone so far that pursuit was useless. They reached the camp of Kalaniopuu at sunset—the last of the Alapa regiment.

"Into the valley of death rode the six hundred." Like sacrifices mark the brave deeds of brave men in all nations.

This battle received the name in Hawaiian history—"The furious destruction at Kakanilua"— Kakanilua was the name of the sand hills below Wai-luku.

Great was the wailing among the royal chiefs of Hawaii and throughout the army. Sore was the heart of the disappointed king. He called a war council of the powerful chiefs of his bodyguard. It was a night council. The old king seemed to have a secret feeling that the gods were fighting against him. Apparently he desired to give up the invasion. He was surrounded by a turbulent band of fighting chiefs. They waged war among themselves when they could not attack the neighbouring islands.

They decided to press on the next day and defeat Kahekili and his allies. Before day began to dawn the camp was roused for action. The majestic masses of clouds almost always hanging over Mt. Iao were glorious in the morning light as the great army drew near the sand hills. The Maui army crowded up toward the steep sides of the mountain as if to avoid the scene of the battle of the preceding day. The debris of battle, the mutilated bodies of hundreds of warriors inspired the great army to endeavour to avenge the recent defeat.

But the Maui army had the advantage of a well chosen position. The Hawaiians had to fight up hill or else drift down to the sand hills. In either case advance was difficult. Each step forward was fully earned. Each sand hill passed was almost as much of a defeat as a victory. There was a full day of savage fighting, marked by inhuman acts of awful brutality. The native account of the battle says: "It was not a war characterised by deeds of princely courtesy." Many noted names of valiant chiefs were never again mentioned in Hawaiian story. The story and the life ended together in this Wailuku battle.

At last the Hawaiian warriors were forced to retreat to the camp of their king, where Kalaniopuu and his guard had waited for the result of the battle.

Kahekili evidently suffered almost as severely as the invaders, for there was scarcely any attempt at pursuit.

Kalaniopuu had brought part of his household with him. His chief queen, Ka-lo-la, was the sister of Kahekili. She had come to share in the victory over her brother and assist in the pacification of her former friends. The attack had been made, and the ragged remnants of a vanquished army had come back.

He was too heavily burdened with camp equipage and suffering men for immediate fight. He proposed that they sue for peace and that his wife, Ka-lo-la, be the messenger to her brother. The queen utterly refused to face her brother. There had been too many past personalities between them, and she had evidently been a vigorous endorser of her husband's invasions into her old homeland. Life was too precious to be risked in that brother's presence. She proposed that the royal prince, Ki-walao, her son, be sent as ambassador.

Kiwalao was robed with all the royal elegance of a king according to the customs of that almost naked, savage life. He wore his finest neck ornaments, his most costly feather cloak and girdle and helmet. He was attended by high chiefs carrying the royal kahili, or large feather banner, and a royal calabash. These chiefs preceded the young prince as his heralds.

When his name and position were announced to the outposts of the Maui army, they fell flat on the face in the sand while he passed by. It was death to stand before a prince or a tabu chief. Kiwalao was one of the highest sacred tabu chiefs in all the islands.

Runners carried the news of the coming of this prince to the Maui king. He was lying on a mat in the royal grass house at Wailuku. Ka-lani-hale

—"the heaven house"—was the name of this home of the king.

As Kiwalao drew near the door all the Maui chiefs prostrated themselves before him, while the king lazily turned over and partly raised himself, lifting his head in token of friendly greeting. To have turned away from the prince, letting his face look down, would have been the sign of immediate death of his visitor. Kiwalao, with slow and dignified tread, crossed the room and seated himself in his uncle's lap. Then both wailed over the troubles which had brought them together, and over the deaths among their followers.

The embassy was successful, and terms of peace between the two kings were arranged. Kalaniopuu returned to Hawaii, to begin at once a new crusade against Kahekili. During the ensuing two years the war degenerated into a series of petty raids by which he kept his wife's brother busy marching warriors from one end of Maui to the other to repel his attacks. In 1779 the coming of Captain Cook changed the course of action and gave the people new things to think about, until Kamehameha secured white men's arms and conquered all the islands.

XIV

THE LAST PROPHET OF OAHU

IN THE DAYS OF KAHAHANA, 1782

PAUMAKUA was one of the great voyagers among the ocean-rovers of over eight hundred years ago. Fornander in his "Account of the Polynesian Race" says: "One of the legends relates that Paumakua, on his return from one of his foreign voyages, brought back with him to Oahu two white men said to have been priests A-ua-ka-hinu and A-ua-ka-mea, afterwards named Kae-kae and Ma-liu, from whom several priestly families in after ages claimed descent and authority." These persons were described as:

"Ka haole nui maka alohilohi
(A large foreigner, bright sparkling eyes)
A aholehole maka aa
(White cheeks, roguish staring eyes)
Ka puaa keokeo nui maka ulaula!
(A great white pig with reddish eyes)."

In the later years of Hawaiian history, two of the most prominent high priests in all the islands were among the descendants of these foreigners. Ka-leo-puu-puu had been high priest of Oahu, but on the death of his king he was superseded by his elder brother, Ka-o-pulu-pulu. He was angry and jealous and gladly welcomed an opportunity to go to Maui as the high priest of Kahekili, the king of Maui. Born on the island of Oahu and belonging to one of the most famous families of priests, he understood thoroughly the temperament of the chiefs of that island and was able to give valuable counsel to his new ruler. He also tried to make as much trouble as possible for his brother Ka-o-pulu-pulu.

It was said that Kahekili followed his advice in creating a division between the king of Oahu and Ka-o-pulu-pulu. He made Kahahana believe that the high priest was secretly hoping to take Oahu from its king and turn it over to himself. This statement was drilled into the mind of the Oahu king while visiting on the island of Molokai. When Kahahana returned to Oahu he did not hesitate to show his enmity toward the high priest. He refused to listen when the priest attempted to give counsel in the meetings of the chiefs. He slighted him in all ways possible and made the fact very evident that he had no confidence in him.

The king not only drove away his high priest, but also estranged his chiefs. It is probable that some of the chiefs rebuked the king for his treatment of such a wise priest and prophet. At any rate the king "became burdensome to the people as well as capricious and heedless."

After nearly two years of distrust and dissension in the court of the king of Oahu, the king of Maui decided to attempt the conquest of his young friend's kingdom. Internal troubles among the chiefs of the island of Hawaii had arisen in connection with the destruction of the Alapa chiefs and Ka-meha-meha's ascent to rulership. There was therefore no danger of an immediate attack from that quarter. Oahu was entirely unsuspicious of danger. The chief difficulty in the way of conquest was the wise and powerful priest Ka-o-pulu-pulu.

The king of Maui sent one of his most trusted servants to Oahu to bring to a climax the enmity of the king toward his priest. This servant came with an appearance of great concern and told Kahahana very confidentially that the priest had once more sent word to the Maui king that he was ready to turn over Oahu to him and aid in the overthrow of Kahahana, but the Maui king felt such great affection for his friend on Oahu that he could not accept such treachery. His feeling, however, was that he ought to warn Kahahana against such a deceitful subject.

The poison again entered into the soul of the king and his anger grew hot within him. He determined that the priest should die. He knew well that he was king by virtue of the choice of his

chiefs and not by blood descent.   He had already
found that his word was not the only law in the
kingdom.   He could not openly declare war against
the priest, but he could command him to render
assistance in worship and sacrifice.   Therefore he
announced that he was intending to journey around
the island for the avowed purpose of consecrating
certain temples and offering sacrifices in others.
As king he had the right to perform those duties in
person, assisted by his priest.

When he had made full preparation he started on
his journey, attended by the usual large train of
servants and companions.   He proceeded as far
as the village Wai-anae on the southwestern coast
of the island.   From Wai-anae the king sent servants with a command to the priest to come to him.

Throughout all the Hawaiian Islands no priest
had a reputation for ability to read the signs of the
sacrifices, utter oracles and prepare incantations
against enemies greater than that of Ka-o-pulu-
pulu.   He was thoroughly skilled in all the deep
mysteries of priestly lore.   He understood the
dread power of "praying to death," a power which
causes even the intelligent natives of the twentieth
century to tremble.

Ka-o-pulu-pulu was fully aware of the enmity
of his king and the danger which attended his
yielding obedience.   He knew also that the plea of
the need of omens and sacrifices was well founded.

To him the future of Oahu looked very dark. He felt that he could not refuse attendance upon the king in this round of public sacrifices. If any opportunity arose for consulting the omens in regard to the future welfare of Oahu it was his duty to give the benefit of his wisdom to his people. It was one more instance of going into the jaws of death for the sake of loyal obedience.

He took his son, Ka-hulu-pue, with him and went to Wai-anae. There he was given no opportunity to offer sacrifice, but was attacked by the servants of the king. The priest's son was forced backward toward the sea. The spirit of prophecy came upon the father as he saw the danger of his son and he gave utterance to one of the oracles for which the Hawaiian priesthood has been noted. He called out to his son: "I nui ke aho a moe i ke kai (it is far better to sleep in the sea), no ke kai ka hoi ua aina" (for from the sea shall come the life of the land). Fornander says that the servants drove the young man into the sea, where he was drowned. The seer no longer felt the compulsion of duty impelling him to seek the king. The king's purpose was evident to all the chiefs and Ka-o-pulu-pulu would not be misjudged if he attempted to escape; therefore he fled eastward toward Honolulu, but was overtaken at Pearl Harbour and killed.

When Kahekili learned of the death of this great

priest he hastened to gather his warriors together and fit out an immense fleet of canoes in order to undertake the conquest of Oahu.

The decisive battle was soon fought and Kahekili secured control over Oahu. Kahahana escaped and for many months wandered over the mountains back of Honolulu, but was at last betrayed and killed.

The oracle of Ka-o-pulu-pulu uttered at the time of the death of his son was kept in the hearts of the natives and its method of fulfilment has been noted. The oracle was easily remembered, although the words concerning the death of his son are repeated in various forms. The oracle reads: "No ke kai ka hoi ua aina" (from the sea comes the life of the land).

When Kahekili landed from his fleet of canoes, and conquered Kahahana, the people said, "The life of the land has come from the sea." Then again when Ka-meha-meha came from Hawaii, conquered Oahu and made Honolulu the centre of his kingdom, the old natives of the island repeated the prophecy and considered it fulfilled.

And yet once more the prophecy was remembered when the foreigners came over the ocean filling the land with new ideas, and with the bustle of new and enlarged business, beautifying and enriching all the island life with new homes and new arts.

XV

THE EIGHT OF OAHU

THIS is a story of one of the most daring deeds in Hawaiian history. After the death of Captain Cook in 1779 Ka-meha-meha was slowly gaining dominion over the large island of Hawaii. Meanwhile the king of Maui, Kahekili, seemed to be far more successful in extending the boundaries over which he exercised rule. Kahekili had control of Maui and the adjacent islands and had sent expeditions to harass the followers of Ka-meha-meha on Hawaii. Oahu was also tempting Kahekili, and he had already taken steps to weaken the forces of that island.

Kahekili had fomented distrust and bloodshed among the Oahu chiefs and at last with an immense fleet of canoes filled with warriors had landed on the beach, south of the crater Leahi, now known as Diamond Head. His canoes were spread along the beach below Diamond Head, covering the sands of Waikiki. This was in the early part of the year 1783.

The King of Oahu had been taken by surprise. He was staying for a time in the beautiful valley back of Honolulu. The Nuuanu stream with its many falls and sweet waters was a place where kings had always loved to rest. While revelling there in seductive pleasures the king, Ka-ha-hana, suddenly was awakened by the report of the coming of the Maui chief. The uninvited guest was unwelcome because no preparation had been made for the reception.

Messengers were hurried to all parts of Oahu, and the warriors were hastily gathered together. Over the mountains and along the arid plains they came. But the force was wofully inadequate to meet the Maui invaders.

In this company there were eight famous warriors, who seemed to think themselves invulnerable. They had often faced danger and returned chanting victory.

The night shadows were falling around the camp when these eight men, one by one, crept away from the other chiefs. Word had been passed from one to the other and a secret expedition partially outlined. Therefore each man was laden with his spear, club, and javelins. When free from all chance of interference they encouraged each other to undertake an expedition, as Fornander says, "on their own account and inflict what damage they could."

Those who have known the Waikiki beach of to-day with its splendidly wooded shores, the luxuriant park inland, the plains covered with trees, and the lower mountain ridges choked with lantana bushes, cannot realise the desolate wastes of the past. The tropical luxuriance of the region around Honolulu belongs to to-day and not to a hundred years ago.

It was over this arid plain dotted here and there by cocoanut trees and across a few streams bordered by taro patches that the eight famous chiefs picked their way. It was not smooth walking. Lava had been poured out from the craters in the mountains and foothills. The softer parts of the petrified streams had dissolved and the surface of the land was covered with the hard fragments which remained. The trail which they followed led in and out among great boulders until they came to the sandy slopes of Diamond Head.

With the coming of morning light they found themselves not far from the old temple, which had been used for ages for most solemn royal ceremonies, a part of which was often the sacrifice of human beings, and here, aided by their gods, they thought to inflict such injuries upon the Maui men as would make their names remembered in the Maui households.

Fornander says: "It was a chivalrous undertaking, a forlorn hope, wholly unauthorised but fully within the spirit of that time for personal valour, audacity, and total disregard of consequences. The names of these heroes were: Pupuka, Makaioulu, Puakea, Pinau, Kalaeone, Pahua, Kauhi and Kapukoa."

Several hundred warriors from Maui were stationed near this temple at the foot of Diamond Head. Probably some of them had carelessly watched the approach of eight chiefs of Oahu. "Into the valley of death rode the six hundred," but this was not an impetuous torrent of six hundred mounted cavalry men sweeping through Russian ranks. It was a handful of eight against what was said to be a force of at least six hundred.

Into these hundreds the eight boldly charged. The conflict was hand to hand, and in that respect was favourable to the eight men well skilled in the use of spear and javelin. Side by side, striking and smiting all before them, the little band forced its way into the heart of the body of its foes. The Maui warriors had expected to take these men, as a fire without trouble swallows up splinters cast into it. They had thought that this little company would afford them an excellent sacrifice for their war gods, and had hoped to take them alive, even at the expense of the lives of a few men. But quickly the formidable character of the eight fighters was appreciated.

Wave upon wave of men from Maui beat against the eight, but each time the wave was shattered and scattered and destroyed. Large numbers were killed while the eight still fought side by side apparently uninjured.

It has been said that this was a fight "to which Hawaiian legends record no parallel." Eight men attacked an army and for some time were victorious in their onslaught.

But the force around them was continually receiving additions, and an overwhelming body of men was slowly crowding over the dead and dying and preparing to crush them by weight of numbers. Then came the whispered call to retreat, and the eight made a terrific onslaught against the circle of warriors surrounding them. It was a marvellous escape. After an awful struggle the opposition was broken down and the eight leaped over the piles of the slain and fled toward the mountains. One of the eight was short and bow-legged. He could fight well, but could not run away as swiftly as his comrades. The Maui men pressed closely after the fleeing chiefs.

The bow-legged man was tripped and thrown. In a moment his spear and javelin were taken from him and a renowned Maui chief caught him and placed him on his back with the face upward, so that he could not do any injury. He started swiftly toward the temple to have his captive sacrificed "as the first victim of the war."

The friends of the captive were still near at hand and heard him cry out that he was captured. They had no hope of being able to rescue him but turned to see if anything could be done. He saw them and called to one of them to kill him rather than let him be sacrificed alive. He urged that a spear be thrown to pierce him through the stomach. "In hope of shortening the present and prospective tortures of his friend, knowing well what his fate would be if brought alive into the enemy's camp, the chief did as he was bidden."

The spear came unerringly toward the prisoner, but as he saw the polished shaft almost piercing him he twisted to one side and it sank deep into the body of the chief who carried him.

In the confusion attendant upon the death of this great chief the bow-legged warrior escaped to his friends and soon all the little company were beyond pursuit.

What became of the eight? Only one lived to perpetuate his name among the families of Oahu. Pupuka became the ancestor of noted chiefs of high rank. The others were probably all killed in the destructive battles which soon followed. Kahekili conquered the Oahu army with great slaughter and finally received the body of Kahahana, which was taken to the temple at Waikiki and offered in sacrifice. After this annihilation of the Oahu army no hint is given of the other members of the band of the famous eight. They live on the pages of history.

XVI

THE RED MOUTH GUN

(KA-PU-WAHA-ULAULA)

THE Red Mouth Gun is the name given by the Hawaiians to the great canoe battle fought off Waipio, Hawaii, in the year 1791, according to Fornander. This was the first naval battle in which guns were the prominent weapons used by the Hawaiian chiefs.

Ka-meha-meha I, in 1789, had gained the adherence of the noted chief Kaiana, who had already visited China and purchased guns and ammunition. This was probably the best stroke of diplomacy exercised by him during all his great work of welding the scattered islands into a united kingdom. Kaiana's real relations were with Kauai rather than Hawaii. In transferring Kaiana's arsenal from Kauai to Hawaii Ka-meha-meha secured an advantage over all the other chiefs of the islands. The man who has material at hand is equipped for any emergency. The possession of this armament led Ka-meha-meha to seize the two white men, Isaac Davis and John Young in the year 1790. These two men were the second great factor in the consolidation of the islands. With arms and ammunition and men skilful in gunnery and wise in counsel Ka-meha-meha was practically invincible.

From this time he dated victories instead of defeats. During the year 1790 he overran Maui and Molokai and subdued a serious rebellion on his own island, Hawaii.

During this conflict at home the high chiefs of the other islands held consultation concerning their common enemy and the best way to overthrow him. They had guns and here and there a white man who had been kidnapped or persuaded to desert from the few ships already visiting the islands. By combining forces it seemed easy to overthrow the high chief of Hawaii. The king of Kauai and the king of Oahu were brothers. Kahekili, the ruler of Oahu, was also the high chief of Maui, which he had placed under the control of his son, Ka-lani-kupule. Therefore the entire northern group of islands was able to combine against Hawaii. It was Ka-meha-meha and one island against the rest of the group.

The natives had used large shells for trumpets. They had a famous war shell known as the "kiha-pu." Anything, therefore, which gave out an explosive noise when blown into was called "pu." When they saw a white man holding a gun to the shoulders, with the resulting smoke and explosion, they gave to the death-dealing magic trumpet the name "pu-waha-ulaula"—the trumpet with the red mouth. Pu became the name for a gun.

The chiefs had massed their forces on Maui. Here Ka-eo-ku-lani, the chief of Kauai, took the leadership of the expedition and, looking upon Maui as redeemed from the victorious inroad of Ka-meha-meha, assumed the island as one of his perquisites of the campaign. Fornander suggests that his older brother, Kahekili, king of Oahu, might have agreed to give him land or even the island as a reward. But here the chiefs of Maui interfered. They were not willing to have the island disposed of in that way. A quarrel arose and the Kauai men attempted to take by force the lands which their high chief claimed and had promised them. Spears were seized, war clubs swung and oval, double-pointed stones dropped into the slings. For a little while there was an exchange of blows. One of the sons of Kahekili, king of Oahu, withstood a large number of Kauai men, holding them at bay unaided. Evidently the quarrel was smoothed over. The Kauai chiefs were never able to again lay any claim to Maui.

The two brothers separated their forces. One fleet of canoes under the Kauai king rendezvoused his boats at Hana, an old and well-known harbour on Maui just across the channel from Hawaii. Hana was the home of some of the most ancient Polynesian legends when applied to the Hawaiian

Islands. The demi-god Maui is said to have noticed how close the sky or clouds came to the earth, and then pushed the sky up until his mother could have room to dry the cloth she was making and the plants have space in which to grow.

When Ka-eo-ku-lani, chief of Kauai, climbed the hills above the seaport he carried his war spear. Standing among the ruins of an ancient fort he threw his spear far up toward the clouds above. Referring to the legends, he cried: "It is said of old that the sky comes close to Hana, but I find it very high. I have thrown my spear and it did not pierce the clouds. I doubt if it will strike Ka-meha-meha. But listen, O you chiefs, warriors and kindred! Be strong and valiant and we shall drink the water of Waipio and eat the taro of Kunaka."

After a little rest the Kauai fleet swept across the channel and passed down the eastern side of Hawaii. The winds of the ocean climb the mountains of Hawaii from the northeast. As they touch the cold surface of the lofty mountain slopes they let fall in heavy showers their burden of waters borne from the sea. Great gulches, bordered by enormous growths of tropical luxuriance, are rapidly formed. Waterfalls hundreds of feet in height shake the falling streams into clouds of spray. Of all these gulches and noted falls on Hawaii, Waipio stands supreme. It was the pride of kings, the sacred home of priests, and the place for the bountiful food supply of royal retinues.

Here the Kauai chief became vandal. He evidently cared but little for the preservation of this, one of the most ancient places on Hawaii. His followers ravaged the taro patches and fish ponds. They seized whatever they wanted for present use and then destroyed the growing plants and broke down protecting banks and walls. To show their contempt for Hawaii they were permitted, and probably commanded by their chief, to tear up and destroy very old and sacred portions of the heiaus, or temples. The ancient palace of Hawaiian kings was supported by sacred posts of pepper tree. These were burned. The palace, of course, was only a large thatched house and could be easily replaced, but the posts, consecrated by the blood of human sacrifices and cared for through many generations, were irretrievably lost.

The natives of Hawaii have a special class of deities known as au-makuas. These are the ghosts of the ancestors watching over the place known in this earthly life, and the family of which they were the progenitors. They were supposed to punish severely any injuries received by those under their care. The people of Hawaii claimed that the Kauai king suffered sorely for his impiety.

Soon Kahekili, chief of Oahu, with the Oahu and Maui war canoes, was driven by Ka-meha-meha from the northwestern coast which they had been devastating. They fled to Waipio and united with the Kauai fleet. Ka-meha-meha had been able to secure some small cannon, which he placed on some of his larger canoes. Isaac Davis and John Young took charge of this portion of battle array. The other canoes were well supplied with firearms. The fleet of the invading army formed in battle array out in the deep waters off the Waipio coast. Here the canoes of Ka-meha-meha found their foes.

In former years a naval battle meant the clash of canoe against canoe, the heavy stroke of war clubs against war clubs and clouds of hurled javelins and spears. The conflict was largely a matter of taunts and shouts, broken canoes and drowning warriors. But in this fight the opposing parties combined the rattle of firearms and the roar of small cannon with the usual war of words. Boats were shattered and the sea filled with swimming men.

The people on the bluffs saw the red flashes of the guns and noted the increasing noise of the artillery until they could no longer hear the voices of men. As the clouds of smoke crept over the sea the battle became, in the view of the watchers, a fight between red mouth guns, and they shouted one to another the news of the progress of the conflict according to the predominance of flashing muskets and cannon. It was soon seen that the invaders were being defeated. The man who had the best arms and the best gunners won the victory.

The Kauai and Oahu kings fled with their scattered fleets to Maui. Ka-meha-meha soon followed them, and during the next three years, step by step, passed over the islands until the kingdom was his.

The death rate during these years of devastating warfare was beyond all calculation and thus came a tremendous decrease in the Hawaiian population.

In the eyes of the old Hawaiians the ghost-gods had avenged themselves in the battle of "the red mouth guns."

XVII

THE LAW OF THE SPLINTERED PADDLE

WOULD you know the story of the Splintered Paddle? It came to pass on the island of Hawaii in the year 1783. It is a true incident in the life of Ka-meha-meha, the great consolidator of the Hawaiian Kingdom.

There are slightly different versions of the tale as frequently occurs when handed down verbally through different channels. The main points are substantially the same. The stalwart king descended to the plane of a highway robber and received his punishment. As a native writer says: "The foundation of the law of the splintered paddle was the greed and shame of a chief dealing with a common man." But, like a true man, Ka-meha-meha made this incident the occasion of a decision to neither commit nor permit any more highway robbery in his kingdom. This then is the outline of the incidents which changed a king into a self-respecting and somewhat law-abiding citizen.

*   *   *   *   *

Two Hawaiian chiefs of splendid physique were hurriedly climbing a zigzag path up the face of an exceedingly steep bluff bordering the little bay of Lau-pa-hoe-hoe. The moment they reached the summit they hastened to the edge that broke in a sheer precipice to the ocean's brink. Eagerly they gazed over the far-reaching waters southward along the banks of the island. "There is no pursuit," said the younger man. "No," replied the elder chief, resting on his spear, "the men of Hilo have crawled back to their homes to heal their wounds. Their war canoes are not among the shadows on the water. Nor do their warriors move along the side of the white mountain (Mauna Kea). Our watchmen do not send the banner of smoke to the sky."

The two chiefs were of high rank. They could both trace their high chief blood through more than a thousand years of royal ancestors. However, the elder chief was of lower rank than the other, because his ancestry had not been guarded with the same jealous care that surrounded the birth of his friend. Among the Hawaiians the "Ahaalii" or "council of nobles" guarded the rank of each chief and assigned to him a place according to the purity of his blood-royal. The younger chief covered his face with his hands and uttered the *Auwe*—the Hawaiian wail for the dead. After a time he raised his head and spoke to his companion, whom we will call Kahai.

"O my Kahai," he said, "yesterday and the defeat at Hilo make my thoughts burn! How do the prophets chant the death of my chiefs and warriors?"

"The singers in the war canoes sang softly, O King, while the boats were hurried along through the night. They sang of our friends whose bodies lie in the ferns. They pronounced curses upon the Hilo chiefs. They called the struggle 'the bitter battle' and that shall be its name in the coming days."

A shudder passed over the young man as he said: "My chiefs no longer lie in the ferns. In my thought I see the temple servants carrying the bodies of my friends to the altars of the gods. It is almost the hour for the evening sacrifice. The hands of the priests are red with blood. The bones of my choice companions will be used for fish hooks. *Auwe-Auwe-e-e!* Woe to me. My name is indeed The Lonely-one—The Desolate!"

"O King! thou art Ka-meha-meha, 'The Lonely One,' the one supreme in royal genealogy, but not 'The Desolate.' Your friends are with you. To-night your war chiefs would die for you. Your prophet has said: 'The cloud of Ka-meha-meha shall rest on the mountains of all the islands.' So shall it be. The gods have said it. Your friends believe it."

Ka-meha-meha (The Only-Only) was an ideal chief. He was over six feet in height, strong and sinewy, excelling all other chiefs in athletic exercises, cruel to enemies, ruling his own household with a rod of iron, generous and brave among his friends, and filled with a fatalistic belief in his own destiny. At heart he was devoted to the interests of his country as far as he understood them. He believed that he knew best, therefore in after years when he became ruler over the group of islands he was thoroughly autocratic. The king's will was to be the people's will. His was a savage face, large-featured, often ferocious and repulsive. On the other hand it was capable of a vast range of playing passions.

His uncle, Ka-lani-opuu, who ruled the large island of Hawaii at the time of the death of Captain Cook, had died in 1782. Ka-meha-meha had been chosen king by a number of influential chiefs in opposition to his cousin Kiwa-lao, the son of Ka-lani-opuu. War arose between the cousins. Kiwa-lao was slain in one of the early conflicts. Other chiefs, of the southern part of the island, refused to swear allegiance to Ka-meha-meha, and had continued the war. The favors of the war gods had been almost equally distributed. The last battle had been fought at Hilo. At the time when our story opens Ka-meha-meha's attack had been repulsed with fearful loss on the part of his followers. At this time he was forty-seven years of age and just commencing the life work of a king and savage statesman.

The king looked thoughtfully down into the valley where the wounded and wearied warriors were

drawing the war canoes out of the inrolling surf.
In the village could be heard wailing as the scanty
news of the battle was hastily reported, and the
people realised that some loved chief or friend
would never return again to their homes.

The king's heart grew warm toward his faith-
ful friends as he want down into the valley to tell
them there was no pursuit, and they could seek
rest and healing.   While the chiefs were around
the poi-bowl that evening he was very quiet.   He
was thinking of the bodies of his warriors laid on
the altars before the gods of the southern districts
of the island.   He thought of the naked altars of
his own Waipio temple, to which he had brought
no captives to be slain in sacrifice.   He imagined
that he might go alone and do some daring deed,
perhaps make a hurried raid upon some unsuspect-
ing point of his enemy's territories.   He rose from
his mat and quietly passed out into the darkness.
He called a few strong boatmen and his favourite
canoe steerer, launched one of the war canoes, and
with sail and paddle sped southward.

That night was rough for Hawaiian seas.   Thunder reverberated in oft-repeated echoes from the
sea cliffs.   Thunder and lightning are rare in this
part of the great Pacific.   Heavy winds blew and
dashed the waves high around the canoe.   The
natives say, "The chief was not in danger, because
his steersman was skilful and watchful.   The sea

did not break over the boat, nor were they wet. Like a dolphin the boat ran over the waves."

It was a misty morning as he passed Hilo Bay, where the greater part of his enemies was encamped. His boat, far out in the shadows, was not noticed. He passed around a corner of the island and planned to surprise the natives of a noted fishing-ground, hoping to make captives and secure booty from some of the warriors against whom the recent battle had been fought.

The morning light was touching the inland mountain tops. It rested, a silver star, on the snowy summit of Mauna Kea. It made a golden glory of the fire clouds of the volcano Kilauea. It glistened over the black beds of pa-hoe-hoe, or smooth, shining lava. It began to bring into strong relief the uplifted heads of the cocoanut trees of a century's growth. The white foam of ocean waves began to be visible along the outer reef.

The natives of Papai, a bay on the Puna coast, hastened into the sea to gather the delicacies which are usually found among the shell-fish along the reef, and also to set nets and snares for fish.

As the mists rose from the waters, the oarsmen entered into the spirit of the adventure. Like a shark the war canoe dashed toward the fishermen.

The people of Puna, looking toward the dawn on the sea, had noticed the boat far out. They asked each other, "What boat is this of the early

morning?" After a little they counted the number of oarsmen. They saw that the newcomers
were strangers. Then they asked a native who was
visiting them, whose home was on the other side
of the island: "O Paiea, do you know who this
is?"

Paiea looked, recognised his ruling chief and
called out: "It is Ka-meha-meha!" Then the
people were filled with fear, for the prowess of
the chief was well known and greatly feared.
They seized paddles and nets and snares and with
the screaming women and children fled, rushing
along the reef, falling into the deep holes, swimming and stumbling toward the mainland.

The king, commanding the others not to follow,
leaped from the canoe to attack two stalwart natives who had been aiding the weak to escape.

The story, related by Kukahi, is that Ka-meha-
meha did not succeed in overtaking any of the
Puna people before they gained the shore and fled
inland. Closely pursuing he called on them to
stop; but with greater terror they continued their
flight. Then he became angry and quickened his
pace. A fisherman turned and threw his fishnet
over the pursuing chief, causing him to fall down
upon the sharp lava. "Blood crawled over the
stones around the fallen body." Then he tore the
nets which entangled him and again rushed heed-
lessly on. While straining himself to see where
the men were running, his foot broke through a

thin shell of lava into a crevice.   To pull it up was impossible.

The men turned back and struck at him with their paddles, but after a few blows the paddles were destroyed.   He managed to grasp a large piece of lava.   The men ran away.   "The thrown stone struck the trunk of a Noni tree, broke it off and with the tree fell to the bottom of a small ravine, and the spot is shown to this day."

The steersman became anxious concerning his chief and came up from the boat.   Meantime the fishermen had secured spears and were returning to kill Ka-meha-meha.   The steersman broke the sharp edges of lava away from the imprisoned foot, but did not succeed in liberating his chief before the natives began to thrust at him with their spears.

The agile chief, fettered as he was, avoided the thrusts, but the steersman was awkward.   One of the spears pierced him.   Ka-meha-meha seized this spear and quickly broke it near the body.   When the men saw that he had a weapon they ran away.

When Ka-meha-meha had freed himself he and his companion came down to the shore.   He warned the men not to repeat the story of the injured man and the battle between himself and the flying fishermen of Puna.   He did not want his high chiefs to know that he had been struck and hurt by a common man.   The chiefs were very strenuous in upholding the dignity of their caste. They thought but little of putting to death their

servants.   That some of the lower classes should
have struck their highest chief was sufficient ground
for killing any of his companions who had failed
to protect him even at the cost of their own lives.

Ka-meha-meha knew how unreasonably wilful
he had been in forbidding his steersman to join
in the pursuit, and therefore felt the injustice of
permitting him to be punished.   It was a weary
journey for the defeated king and his wounded
steersman.

The spear-head and part of the shaft still rested
in the side of the wounded man.   The king could
not have the spear removed without great danger,
so waited, thinking to have the wound well cared
for after reaching Lau-pa-hoe-hoe.   However, it
was impossible to keep the boatmen from telling
the story of the splintered paddle and the wounded
steersman.   The chiefs soon heard the particulars
and called the council of chiefs.   There they grimly
voted to "heal" the wounded man.

Ka-meha-meha appealed to them:

"O chiefs!   The night of our going away was
a very evil night.   There was storm and wind and
thunder; yet I received no injury, nor was I even
wet by the sea.   Nor was I permitted to feel the
least fear.   My steersman was wise and skilful.
He was my close friend on the deceitful and dangerous sea.   Therefore I ask you, if you wish to
see him healed, have him brought before my eyes
for the treatment."

But some of the chiefs went out and instead of bringing the wounded man into the council took him and twisted the spear-point, pulling it back and forth, until he died.

After Ka-meha-meha returned from his Puna excursion he rested for a time. His adventure was not encouraging. He decided that he could not hasten the plans of the gods. The ancient Hawaiian was very much of a fatalist. So also is the Hawaiian of to-day. What has to be is accepted without rebellion.

Ka-meha-meha realised that he was too weak, both in personal strength and in the number of warriors, to make further effort for the time being. Therefore, he sent his warriors home to cultivate their fields and prepare new war material for future conflicts.

While this preparation was going on, a new element entered into Hawaiian warfare. The white man's ships and the white man's weapons were becoming familiar to the great king.

White men were secured to take charge of small cannon, and to drill squads of warriors equipped with the rude firearms of a century ago.

Some of these white leaders and their muskets found their way into the service of almost all the important chiefs throughout the islands.

Ka-meha-meha owned the best harbours and offered the best inducements for trade with the foreigners. He secured the best equipment of arms and men. This gave Ka-meha-meha a vast advantage over the antagonistic kings and chiefs of his own and other islands. He had large boats built and armed with small swivel cannon. He had sixteen foreigners in his service. He led his victorious warriors from island to island. In his last campaign it is said his fleet of canoes lined the beach of one of the islands for a distance of four miles.

In a few years his friends saw the prophecy fulfilled. "His cloud was resting on the mountains of all the islands." He had unified the group under one autocratic government, and had established the Ka-meha-meha dynasty.

Then came the memory of that excursion made in 1783 to Puna for the sake of robbery and possible murder. The king wondered what had become of the men who had attacked him. He had gone to Hilo and was having a fine fleet of wide and deep canoes made in the splendid koa forests back of Hilo. While waiting here, some time between the years 1796 and 1802, he determined to find the men of the splintered paddle. He knew that these men might have changed their residence from the Puna district to Hilo. So he sent messengers throughout both districts summoning all the people to a great meeting in Hilo. Certain large grass houses were set apart for the large assembly. The Hilo people were separated from

HAWAIIAN GRASS HOUSES

the families of the other district. When the people were thus gathered together they found themselves prisoners. They feared wholesale destruction. The days of human sacrifices among the Hawaiians had not passed by. The new king, against whom they had at one time fought, might intend their sacrifice in numbers. They were his property to be burned or cut to pieces and placed in the temples of the gods. No one could dispute the will of the chief. It was a political condition which the Hawaiians of a hundred years later could scarcely begin to realise. That man is very ignorant who thinks the old days best.

The king passed through the houses allotted to the Hilo people. It must have been an anxious time for the prisoners. Wholesale destruction, possibly because of the bitter war of 1783, stared them in the face. But the chief touched them not and passed through their lines out to the houses in which the Puna people were confined.

A suspicion at least of the reason for their imprisonment must have come to the guilty men. The story runs that when they saw Ka-meha-meha they bowed their heads, hoping to escape recognition. But this revealed them at once to Ka-meha-meha, and he approached them with the command to raise their heads. It was an interesting scene when these common men were brought before the chiefs for final judgment. It is said the chief asked them if they were not at the sea of Papai. They assented. Then came the question to two of them:

"You two perhaps are the men who broke the paddle on my head?"

They acknowledged the deed.

"To the death, to the death!" cried the chiefs around the king.

"Down the face!" "Command the stones!" "Let the man and his friends be stoned to death!"

The king listened to the suggestions of his companions. Then he said: "Listen! I attacked the innocent and the defenceless. This was not right. In the future no man in my kingdom shall have the right to make excursions for robbery without punishment, be he chief or priest. I make the law, the new law, for the safety of all men under my government. If any man plunders or murders the defenceless or the innocent he shall be punished. This law is given in memory of my steersman and shall be known as 'Ke Kana-wai Ma-mala-hoa,' or the law of the friend and the broken oars. The old man or the old woman or the child may lie down to sleep by the roadside and none shall injure them."

The law with the name Ma-mala-hoa is still on the statute books of Hawaii. It has been greatly modified and enlarged, but the decree against robbery by any man, and especially the plunder of the weak by the powerful, had its beginning for Hawaii in the days of Ka-meha-meha.

Alexander says in his history of the islands: "During the days of Ka-meha-meha energetic measures were taken for the suppression of brigandage, murder and theft throughout the kingdom."

"The Law of the Splintered Paddle" marked the awakening of a pagan conscience to a sense of just dealing between the strong and the weak.

XVIII

LAST OF THE TABU

TO-DAY the thatched house is a curiosity in the Hawaiian Islands. In the time of our story the grass roof was the only shelter from the rain and heat, except the thick-leaved tree or the insecure lava cave. The long rushes and grasses from the sea marshes and the long leaves of the pandanus tree made a very good if not a very enduring home. There the chiefs and common people alike were born, and out of such grass houses their bodies were carried when life was over.

It was the same story told over again on islands or continents. The chief's house might have a few more mats of a little finer texture, or calabashes of wood with markings a little more unique, but birth nights left fully as many beautiful children, and the hours of death took away fully as many noble men and women from the poor hut built by the taro patch as from the better-apportioned home under the silver-leaved kukui or candle-nut tree. Out of the ranks of the unappreciated have come some of the best people of the earth, and some of the strongest influences changing nations.

There was a modest grass house in one of the upland valleys of Kailua, Hawaii. Tall cocoanut trees bent over it. Near it grew the ohia, or native apple tree, luxuriant in crimson tassel-like blossoms. The sacred ohelo berries ripened in the iliahi or sandalwood forest above.

One bright afternoon a tall, finely formed woman broke through the arching branches which obstructed the path and approached the door where an old woman sat crooning to a child resting in her arms. The old woman looked up, and then fell on her face, crying:

"Oh! my chief! my chief! My Ka-ahu-manu!"

The queen gently raised the old woman, calling her "mother," as was the Hawaiian custom when speaking to favourite retainers.

"Where are Oluolu and her husband?" asked the queen.

"Coming soon with the pink taro you so dearly love," was the reply.

While the favourite queen of Ka-meha-meha was visiting with her old nurse, a happy young couple came from the near-by taro patch. The young man carried a bunch of rare bananas. When he saw the queen he prostrated himself at her feet and, without thinking, gave the bananas to her.

Ka-ahu-manu laughed gaily, saying: "O my thoughtless one, you have tempted your queen to break tabu."

A horrified expression crossed his face and he hastily started to withdraw the bananas. But the queen was wayward and self-willed. Her hand was on the bunch as she said:

"This is mine. It is your offering to your chief. I will eat of these bananas." In a moment she was eating the delicious fruit.

Then the old woman began to wail: "Auwe, auwe! The queen must die and we shall all be destroyed!"

"Hush, mother," said the young man, as he glanced significantly over to Oluolu, who had evidently some secret knowledge of the way to violate tabu. "Many people think that the tabu is not right, and that the threatened punishments come not from the gods, but from the priests themselves. The white men in Ka-meha-meha's court do not keep tabu, nor do they die. Even the king does not require human sacrifices. Old things are passing away."

"But the gods will punish the people for the growing unbelief," murmured the grandmother.

"Not if the belief is false," said Oluolu.

Ka-ahu-manu listened in astonishment. She had done many things secretly which she did not care to have come to the ears of the priests, but she could scarcely believe that the common people did the same. She said:

"Is this the talk of the common people?"

"No," answered Oluolu. "Only a few speak

freely one to another.   The dread of the priest is over the land."

When Ka-ahu-manu returned to the king's houses she kept these things in her heart.   She saw the priests and their spies becoming more vigilant and more violent.   She realised that the foreigners were exerting a strong influence against the tabu system.   Her outspoken speeches, for which the priests did not dare to punish her, were bearing fruit.   The indignation of the queens of Ka-meha-meha was aroused when a priest commanded that a little girl who had been caught eating bananas should have one of her eyes gouged out.   Then came a carousal, after which a tipsy woman stumbled into her husband's eating-house and was put to death for violating the tabu.   Ka-ahu-manu talked these and many other similar experiences over when she visited the old grass house, gaining new ideas and new confidence from her loyal retainers; but the old woman, with aching heart, sat in the door, muttering incantations to keep her queen and her children from the danger which their words seemed to invite.

Ka-meha-meha died about 2 o'clock in the morning of May 8, 1819.   When he knew that his illness was serious he gave the kingdom jointly to Ka-ahu-manu and his son, Liho-liho.

The very morning of Ka-meha-meha's death some chiefs came to Ka-ahu-manu with the proposition that she use her authority and declare the tabu at an end. But there was an indescribable scene of riotous confusion and revelry and lust. Even the ordinary restraints of savage society were laid aside. Priests were occupied with signs and incantations to discover some one who might have prayed the great king to death. Ka-ahu-manu's party of practical unbelievers were under suspicion. Therefore the queen decided that the time had not yet come to take such an eventful step. However, some of the people violated different tabus and suffered no injury. Kee-au-moku, the queen's brother, broke the tabu staff of the priests, and Hewa-hewa, the high priest, later gave his influence not only toward the suppression of the tabus, but also toward the destruction of the idols and their temples.

After a few days Liho-liho, the young king, and Ka-ahu-manu, in their most regal apparel, met and together assumed the government of the Hawaiian Islands. At that time Ka-ahu-manu proposed that they henceforth disregard the tabus. But the king, although under the influence of liquor, was not quite ready to take this step. Some of the chiefs also opposed such action. Keopuolani, one of the queens, asked the king to eat with her. But Liho-li-ho delayed the answer. Then she took his little brother (afterward Ka-meha-meha III) and induced him to eat with her. This gave an example of the most sacred tabu chief in the land violating tabu with her little son. Soon the king yielded and openly ate and drank with the queens at a feast in which many tabu articles were placed. The word passed rapidly from island to island, and was hailed with joy by the mass of the people.

But the guardian of the war god, Kaili, felt responsibility placed upon him by the dying charge of Ka-meha-meha. He felt that it was his high trust to protect the tabus and the worship of the gods. He was strong and fearless. The priests and chiefs who wished to perpetuate tabu gathered around him and a rebellion was instituted.

The story of the "battle of Kua-moo" must be told very briefly. It was the death struggle of the fanatics. It was the attack of the handful upon the better armed and larger army. It was a long drawn-out conflict. At last the guardian of the war god, wounded and bleeding, fought, seated upon a block of lava. By his side his wife stood, also fighting bravely. As he, struck by a musket ball, fell back dead, she cried out: "I surrender!" But at that moment a ball struck her in the temple and she fell dead by the body of her husband.

How the tabus were laid aside, the idols destroyed and the temples burned—all this is a matter of history. But no writer has chronicled how the young husband carried the news from Kailua to the grass house under the cocoanut trees. No one has written of the joy of Oluolu in the life of broader privileges secured by abolishing the tabu system. And no one has described the old woman who could not understand the new order of things, but sat in the door of the grass house in the valley and grieved over the shattered doctrines of her forefathers.

XIX

FIRST HAWAIIAN PRINTING

FOREIGNERS from all over the world called on the Hawaiians and remained with them forty years before the missionaries came. Their influence was negative. They did not study the people or help them to study. John Young, Don Marin and Isaac Davis were notable exceptions in a few things, but the fact remains that no earnest effort was made by any one to help the natives intellectually until the missionaries came.

Alexander Campbell, who, in 1809, was left in Honolulu by a whaling ship on account of frozen feet, revealed the situation. The king Tamaahmaah (Ka-meha-meha) ordered Boyd, his carpenter, to make a loom for Campbell to use in weaving cloth for sails. Boyd declined, saying, "The natives should be taught nothing that would render them independent of strangers."

Campbell places on record the feeling among the foreigners. "When a brother of the Queen's, whose name I do not remember—but who was usually called by the white people John Adams—wished me to teach him to read, Davis would not permit me, observing, 'They will soon know more than ourselves.' " It is interesting to note that Gov. Adams, whose native name was Kuakini, did learn to read and write under the missionaries and has left two short letters, in both of which he presents a request for saws.

In one he says, "My wife is going away to Hawaii. If perhaps she can carry, give you to me sahs tools," signed "Gov. Adams." In the other letter he says he is building a house and wants a "sah tool" which he will return when the work is done.

The missionaries landed at Kailua on the island Hawaii, April 4, 1820, and there divided their party, the larger number coming to "Hanaroorah, Honolulu, April 19."

Mr. Bingham says, "They began at once to teach.—The first pupils were the chiefs and their favourite attendants and the wives and children of foreigners." The first instruction was necessarily in English, but the missionaries used every opportunity to become acquainted with the speech of the people and make it a written language. They wrote down as carefully as they could every new word which came to their ears. This was no small task and was absolutely necessary as the foundation of a written language.

As soon as the missionaries were sure of the orthography and pronunciation of a number of words they prepared a primer or spelling book to be

THE ALPHABET.

—◆—

VOWELS. Names.	SOUND. Ex. in Eng.	Ex. in Hawaii.
A a --- â	as in *father*,	la—sun.
E e --- a	— *tete*,	hemo—cast off.
I i --- e	— *marine*,	marie—quiet.
O o --- o	— *over*,	one—sweet.
U u --- oo	—*rule*,	nui—large.

CONSONANTS.	Names.	CONSONANTS.	Names.
B b	be	N n	nu
D d	de	P p	pi
H h	he	R r	ro
K k	ke	T t	ti
L l	la	V v	vi
M m	mu	W w	we

The following are used in spelling foreign words:

F f	fe	S s	se
G g	ge	Y y	yi

1

FIRST LEAFLET PRINTED, 1822

printed for the schools they were carrying on. Mr. Bingham says: "On the 7th of January, 1822, we commenced printing the language in order to give them letters, libraries and the living oracles in their own tongue. A considerable number was present, and among those particularly interested was Ke-au-moku (Gov. Cox) who after a little instruction by Mr. Loomis applied the strength of his athletic arm to the lever of a Ramage press, pleased thus to assist in working off a few impressions of the first lessons."

Although these impressions were merely proof sheets, probably, of the first half of the spelling book, yet the large number printed and put in use, nearly 100 in all, would make this the first item printed.

This was the first printing done in the Hawaiian islands and along the North Pacific coast west of the Rocky Mountains. These first sheets created a new interest among the chiefs. King Liho-liho (Ka-meha-meha II) visited the press, saw a sheet of clean white paper laid over the type, then "pulled the lever around and was surprised to see the paper instantly covered with words in his own language."

While the chiefs were awakened by these proof impressions to intellectual desires never before experienced, the work was being pushed of finishing the second "signature" and the complete book of sixteen pages was printed in an edition of 500 copies. Gov. Adams (Kuakini) secured one of the first copies of these lessons "and was quickly master of them."

Liho-liho was glad to have the chiefs instructed and took 100 copies of the first primer for his friends and attendants. Ka-ahu-manu took 40 for her friends. These probably came from this printing of 500 copies. In the latter part of September, another printing of 2,000 copies was made from the same type.

Liho-liho felt a little like the foreigners who did not want the natives instructed. He wanted the education reserved for the chiefs because, according to Mr. Bingham, "he would not have the instruction of the people in general come in the way of their cutting sandalwood to pay his debts."

Nevertheless, the flood could not be held back and the privilege of reading and writing rapidly spread among the people. In six years there was the record—

"Oahu: Mission Press, Nov. 1828; 5 Ed.; 20,-000. Total, 120,000."

Meanwhile a great deal of other printed matter had been issued from that first press.

March 9, 1822, at the request of the king and high chiefs a handbill, entitled, "Port Regulations," was printed, probably to aid the rulers in quieting the differences which were continually arising with sea captains. The fourth item recorded as issued in these islands was in December, 1823, and is the very rare and unique little book of 60 pages of

NA

HIMENI HAWAH;

HE ME

ORI IA IEHOVA,

KE

AKUA MAU.

*E hoonani ia IEHOVA, e oukou na aina
a pau: e hoorea ia Ia e oukou na kanaka
a pau.*—Davida.

—

OAHU:

PANA I KA MEA PAI PALAPALA A KA
POE MISIONARI.
1823.

TITLE PAGE OF FIRST HYMN BOOK, 1823

Hawaiian hymns prepared by Rev. Hiram Bingham and Rev. William Ellis, an English missionary from Tahiti who resided in Honolulu at the time, heartily allying himself with the American missionaries. His previous knowledge of the similar language of Tahiti made it easy for him to learn Hawaiian. The edition of this hymn book was 2,000 copies.

The most interesting part of the story of printing in the Hawaiian Islands belongs to the greatest work accomplished for the good of the people— the printing of the Bible in the Hawaiian language. This article has space for only a few facts. The first printed Bible passage was in a revised spelling book published April, 1825. This was John 3, 16-21. Then in June, 1825, a booklet, 4 pages, called—"He olelo a ke Akua," or "Selected Scriptures," was probably printed on the same demy with "He ui," or "A catechism," 8 pages—each 7,000 copies. In November, 1825, the hundredth Psalm was "printed on a card for the opening of the church built by Ka-lai-moku at Honolulu," then in December, 1825, the Ten Commandments and the Lord's Prayer; in July, 1826, the Good Samaritan, and in January, 1827, the Sermon on the Mount.

In December, 1827, came the first systematic attempt toward printing the Bible. Twelve pages of the Gospel of Luke were struck off—10,700 copies. Later the entire book of Luke was printed in Honolulu. The other gospels, Matthew, Mark and John, were printed in 1828 in the United States. A copy of these three gospels, bound in an elegant and substantial cover, was presented to Ka-pio-lani, the high chiefess who defied Pele on the brink of the pit-crater of Kilauea in 1825. This volume now lies in the archives of the Hawaiian Board. The entire Bible was completed and "the finishing sheet was struck off May 10, 1839."

An interesting prophecy concerning the completion of the Bible is found in a writing book, where, under the date April 30, 1827, is the record of a conversation. Mr. Bingham says that it is the duty of the mission to complete a translation of the Bible in five years from this time and thinks that with circumstances as favourable as they now are it will be done.

Mr. Whitney says: "I say if the whole Bible is in print in the Hawaiian language in ten years from this time it is as much as I expect, and I think will be a progress exceeding that of any other mission to any heathen country having a language not previously written or reduced to order." It was a little over twelve years after the first pages were prepared before the complete Bible was in print.

KA
EUANELIO
A LUKA:
OIA KA MOO OLELO HEMOLELE,
NO KO KAKOU HAKU E OLA I,
NO
IESU KRISTO;
I LAWEIA
I OLELO HAWAII.

"I loaa Ona ke ola, he malamalama ke ola no na kanaka."

OAHU:
I PAIIA MA KA MEA PAI PALAPALA A KA POE MISIONARI.
1827.

FIRST BIBLE PRINTING, 1827
GOSPEL OF LUKE

XX

THE FIRST CONSTITUTION

MANY subtle influences were at work in the evolution of Hawaiian civilisation. Between the years 1835-1840 there was a culmination of several forces, each one important in itself and all uniting to bring about the exceedingly interesting series of events which marked the Hawaiian history of that time. Missionary instruction commenced in 1820. The work of translating the Bible into the Hawaiian language was completed and the book published in 1839. For several years the thoughts of the Bible had been studied and preached with great clearness and power as the result of the labour of translating and criticising the different books. Then came one of the most remarkable religious revivals in history. These years of religious instruction, with their resultant awakening of conscience and yearning for a better life, could not escape a close connection with the contemporaneous demands of civilisation. The double development could not be separated.

During these same years there came a new relation to the larger nations of the world. International complications succeeded each other with great rapidity. A controversy with Roman Catholic priests, much as it was deprecated by the missionaries, was nevertheless a very useful factor in making the king and chiefs realise that they must be better prepared to deal with foreign interference. There was plain necessity for a knowledge of law and government. Schools and churches and the first newspapers published in the Pacific Ocean were all enforcing the demand for better government.

In 1833 King Ka-meha-meha III was thinking seriously of holding unbridled sway over his people. Alexander says that he "announced to his chiefs his intention to take into his possession the land for which his father had toiled, the power of life and death, and the undivided sovereignty." His purpose was to have no government distinct from the will of the king.

The earthquake changes in civil conditions occurring at that time throughout the islands speedily made the king and the chiefs conscious of their ignorance of methods of government, and in 1836 they applied to the United States "for a legal adviser and instructor in the science of government." This was a request difficult to grant speedily. In 1838 the right man for the place was selected from among the American missionaries in the islands. His name was William Richards. Under his instruction an outline of forms of civil government was rapidly given to the leading men of the kingdom. Ka-meha-meha III determined to put the lessons into practice, and in 1839 issued what he called "A Declaration of Rights—Both of the People and the Chiefs," and in October, 1840, promulgated the first Constitution of the Hawaiian Islands, quickly following these documents with a code of laws agreed to unanimously by the council of chiefs and signed by both the king and his premier.

These laws and the Constitution and Declaration of Rights were first published in English in 1842. The Declaration and Constitution owe much of their remarkably clear and broad conceptions of the relation of ruler and subject to Mr. Richards. Nevertheless, it is a somewhat remarkable fact that men of such limited civilisation as the king and chiefs should have been willing to voluntarily give up so large a use of power as is marked in the adoption of such a radically new form of government as arose in 1839-1840. It was a revolution of ideas and purposes and customs remarkable in its extent and thoroughness.

Laws had been made by kings and chiefs as far back as the year 1823. Many difficulties had been decided according to the tabu, or practices of the chiefs, or according to the general principles of common law. The established customs of civilised nations had considerable force in disputes between natives and foreigners. But at last the rulers of the land began to put their government into permanent shape. Mr. Richards had much to do in the preparation of the new system of rule. The foreign consuls assisted and even wrote some of the earlier laws. Commanders of warships made suggestions. Missionaries were consulted. David Malo, John and Daniel Ii and other pupils of the early missionaries wrote some of the original laws. The king and the high chiefs ratified these laws, explained them to the people and put them in force. This is in brief the situation immediately preceding and accompanying the peaceable and yet irreclaimable establishment of constitutional rights and privileges in Hawaii.

Three steps are to be noticed in the growth of the recognition of the rights of the common people. The Declaration of Rights, the Constitution, and the Enactment of Laws by an elected legislature. Once taken, no royal will could ever retrace these steps. The king and his chiefs made a gulf between their past and their future history and could not bridge it or re-cross it. The Hawaiian Magna Charta, like that of King John Lackland, was irrevocable, because, like the great charter of England, it was a step in the evolution of human liberty. It is interesting to note the similarity of thought and language when the leading principle of the Magna Charta is placed beside the supreme gift of the king granted in the Hawaiian Declaration of Rights.

What has been called "The essence and glory of Magna Charta" reads as follows: "No freeman shall be taken, or imprisoned, or dis-seized, or outlawed, or banished, or anyways injured, nor will we pass upon him, nor send upon him, unless by the legal judgment of his peers or by the law of the land."

The Hawaiian Declaration of Rights, issued June 7, 1839, stated first the principle upon which the American Declaration of Independence was founded, viz.:

"That God has bestowed certain rights alike on all men, and all chiefs, and on all people of all lands."

Then the further fundamental principle was outlined that:

"In making laws for the nations, it is by no means proper to enact laws for the protection of the rulers only, without also providing protection for their subjects."

Then came the necessary conclusion, which is very similar to the crux of Magna Charta:

"Protection is hereby secured to the persons of all the people, together with their lands, their building lots, and all their property while they conform to the laws of the kingdom, and nothing whatever shall be taken from any individual, except by express provision of the laws."

In order to carry out this Declaration of Rights Ka-meha-meha III and his high chiefs were led irresistibly to the promulgation of a Constitution which should differentiate the functions of the different branches of government and provide for a proper presentation of the needs of the people. As surely as the sunlight follows the morning star so certainly came the provision for a House of Nobles representing the chiefs and a House of Representatives representing the people.

The Constitution was promulgated October 8, 1840. After reiterating the Declaration of Rights the king defines the legislative, executive and judicial branches of government and establishes the legislature and bestows upon it the power of enacting laws. Previously he had enacted law with the advice of his council of high chiefs.

The laws which were passed after this Constitution was promulgated are both curious and instructive. There is a very large concession on the part of the king and the high chiefs who constituted his advisers, and a correspondingly large increase of privileges on the part of the common people. This is especially noticeable in the enactment of laws concerning taxation. Before the days of the Constitution and legislature the king held all power in his own hands, although the *Aha-alii,* or Council of Chiefs, was a factor with which he continually reckoned. The common people were not taken very much into account before the influence of Christianity was felt by both king and chiefs.

In the act of the Legislature and House of Nobles signed by the king November 9, 1840, three forms of taxation are specified—the poll tax, the land tax, and the labour tax.

The poll tax could be paid in arrowroot, cotton, sugar or anything which had a specific money value. The most important exemption looked toward the preservation of large families. "If any parents have five, six, or more children, whom they support . . . then these parents shall by no means be required to pay any poll, land or labour tax until their children are old enough to work, which is at fourteen years of age."

The land tax was to be paid in swine.

If lands were forfeited they were to go back into the hands of the king, "and he shall give them out again at his discretion, or lease them, or put them into the hands of those who have no lands, as he shall think best."

The labour tax would be considered an exceedingly heavy burden by the public of the present time and yet that labour law was very much less oppressive than the semi-civilisation which preceded it. The native who sighs for the return of the days of the olden time would speedily try to get back out of the fire into what he considers a frying pan. Twelve days' public labour out of every month would be considered exceedingly oppressive if exacted by the government of to-day. Yet thus reads a part of the enactment of 1840:

"When public labour is to be done of such a

nature as to be a common benefit to king and people, and therefore, twelve days in a month are devoted to labour; then all persons, whether connected with the land or not, and also all servants shall go to the work or pay a fine of half a dollar a day."

Fines were exacted from the late and lazy. The man coming after 7 o'clock in the morning was fined an eighth of a dollar, and after dinner a fourth of a dollar. While the man who was lazy and idle one day was fined two days' extra labour. There were, of course, exemptions for infirmity, large families and other good reasons.

There was enacted a special law for the lazy and worthless element of the community.

The words of the law seem to come from the lips of the king. "As for the idler, let the industrious man put him to shame, and sound his name from one end of the country to the other." The chiefs were exhorted "to disperse those lazy persons who live in hordes around you, through whom heavy burdens are imposed upon your labouring tenants." "Treat with kindness those who devote their strength to labour, till their tattered garments are blown about their necks, while those who live with you in indolence wear the clean apparel for which the industrious poor have laboured."

It is well known that laws are applied sermons, but these laws are sometimes primarily sermons, as the introduction to Act III well says: "A portion of this law is simply instruction and a portion is direct law. That part which simply disapproves of certain evils is instruction. If a penalty is affixed that is absolute law." Hence the following exhortations are made to the chiefs: "That the land agents and that lazy class of persons who live about us should be enriched to the impoverishment of the lower classes, who with patience toil under their burdens, is not in accordance with the designs of this law. This law condemns the old system of the king, chiefs, land agents and tax officers. That merciless treatment of common people must end."

It is worthy of notice that the fourth act of these early laws practically recognised the New England system of "local" or "town" government. The words are peculiar, "If the people of any village, township, district, or state consider themselves afflicted by any particular evils in consequence of there being no law which is applicable . . . then they may devise a law which will remedy their difficulties. If they shall agree to any rule, then that rule shall become a law for that place, but for no other." This was to apply especially to any community's desire concerning fences, animals at large, and roads. "Though no such law can be at variance with the general spirit of the laws of the nation nor can there be any oppressive law nor one of evil tendency."

In 1842 an act was signed by the king and the

premier, in which the evident intent is a lesson for the common people—a lesson to be enforced by contrasts. "The people are wailing on account of their present burdens. Formerly they were not called burdens. Never did the people complain of burdens until of late. This complaint of the people, however, would have a much better grace if they with energy improved their time on their own free days; but lo! this is not the case. They spend their days in idleness, and therefore their lands are grown over with weeds and there is little food growing. The chiefs, of their own unsolicited kindness, removed the grievous burdens. The people did not first call for a removal of them. The chiefs removed them of their own accord. Therefore the saying of some of the people that they are oppressed is not correct. They are not oppressed, but they are idle."

For that reason a new law was enacted stating that it "shall be the duty of the tax officer whenever he sees a man sitting idle or doing nothing on the free days of the people (*i. e.,* the days, when they were not required to work for the king or chiefs) to take that man and set him at work for the government, and he shall work till night."

Accompanying this act compelling idlers to toil there was a clear statement of the strong contrast between the burdens of the time immediately preceding and those after the passage of the new laws. These changes are worth noting because of their historical bearing upon the past and present condition of the native Hawaiians.

"Formerly if the king wished the property of any man he took it without reward, seized it by force or took a portion only, as he chose, and no man could refuse him. The same was true of every chief and even the landlords treated their tenants thus." This was so changed that if a chief should attempt it "he would instantly cease to be a chief on this archipelago."

"Formerly the chief could call the people from one end of the islands to the other to perform labour." "If the king wished the people to work for him they could not refuse. They must work from month to month. So also at the call of every chief and every landlord."

"Formerly if the people did not go to the work of the king when required, the punishment was that their houses were set on fire and consumed." The fact must be recognised that before the adoption of this Constitution under the influence of the American missionaries the common people never owned any land or had any especial rights.

The power of the king and chiefs up to the time of their freely giving this constitution and new set of laws was practically unlimited. The fact that they voluntarily limited themselves for the benefit of the people must be noted to the credit of an awakened conscience under missionary guidance.

XXI

THE HAWAIIAN FLAG

THE flag which has floated over the Hawaiian Islands for more than a century is a combination of the "Union Jack" and stripes rather than the "Stars and Stripes," to which it now gives precedence. The Union Jack in the upper or "halyard" corner, and eight stripes, red, white and blue, constitute the old flag of Hawaii.

This flag has a story worth hearing.

Vancouver visited the "Sandwich Islands" with Captain Cook. Nearly fifteen years later he returned in command of an expedition. February 21, 1794, he entered into an agreement with Ka-meha-meha I and his Council of Chiefs to receive the islands under the protection of Great Britain. February 25, with great ceremony, the English flag was raised over Ka-meha-meha's royal home on the island of Hawaii. Probably this flag was the first "Union Jack" adopted by King James, 1603-1625, on the political union of England and Scotland.

This flag was succeeded in 1801 by the present Union Jack, which is made by placing three crosses upon a blue field—St. George's of England, a red cross; St. Andrew's of Scotland, a white cross, and St. Patrick's of Ireland. The Irish addition to the flag consisted of St. Patrick's red cross laid upon St. Andrew's white cross, and half covering it. This was the second Union Jack. The name "Jack" is said to have come from the red cross on the "jacque"—the coat of mail or outer coat of the soldiers of England.

The second Union Jack was the second flag to float authoritatively over the Hawaiian Islands. The fact that Ka-meha-meha placed the English flag over his government has sometimes been construed as a technical "cession of the islands to the English crown." But the astute Ka-meha-meha, while looking for English protection from the greed of other nations, stipulated that the Hawaiians should "govern themselves in their own way and according to such laws as they themselves might impose." The action of Vancouver was not ratified in England, owing to more important European questions, and a real protectorate was never established. Nevertheless, there was a nominal guardianship afforded by the presence of the English flag floating over the Hawaiian grass houses and fleets of boats.

It should be said that during preceding centuries each high chief had carried a pennant of coloured native cloth at the masthead of his double war canoe, but these were individual and family rather than national banners.

At first the English flag was established only upon the island of Hawaii. Then it passed with Ka-meha-meha from island to island as he conquered the high chiefs and became the sole ruler of the group. When the king made Honolulu his chief royal residence the flag floated over his house near the seashore. On Kauai, the island farthest north of all the group, there was a strong Russian influence. The Russians built a fort at the mouth of one of the rivers. Against their armed possession of any part of the islands King Ka-meha-meha made strong objection, but, according to the statements of sailors, the Russian flag was used by the high chief of Kauai until finally displaced by the Hawaiian flag.

The English flag over Honolulu was a warning to other nations, and also to lawless individuals. No man could tell exactly how far to go in the presence of that flag. The sailors of those days unquestionably ran riot in wickedness, and the early influences of white civilisation were absolutely awful. But there was a limit beyond which the lawless element did not dare to pass. The flag would permit England to advance whatever claim might be desired in case of any great trouble.

This continued from 1794 to 1812. Then war broke out between England and the United States. Alexander, in a report to the Hawaiian Historical Society, says that upon the outbreak of this war a friendly American persuaded Ka-meha-meha I "to have a flag of his own."

An English Captain (George C. Beckley) some time near the beginning of the century brought a small ship to the islands and sold it to the chiefs. He then settled in Honolulu and became a friend of the king, who made him a "tabu-chief." He married an Hawaiian woman of high priestly family. Nevertheless, "she had to kolo-kolo or crawl on her hands and knees whenever she entered the house of her husband, the tabu-chief."

To Captain Beckley was entrusted the task of designing and making the first Hawaiian flag. The pattern flag, the first one made, was afterward "fashioned into a child's frock and worn on special occasions by each one of the children in succession, and was long preserved as an heirloom in the family."

This was apparently a compromise between the flags of the two antagonistic English-speaking nations. The Jack was retained to show the king's friendship for England. The stripes were said to represent the red, white and blue of the American flag. They were eight in number, to represent the eight principal islands of the group. It was a combination of Hawaiian with European and American interests.

The old king was very proud of his beautiful new flag, and displayed it from his palace and over

the royal homes in other islands. It superseded
the Russian flag on Kauai. He built a new coral
rock fort, 300 x 400 feet dimensions, with walls
twelve feet high and twenty feet thick. In it he
placed forty guns, six, eight and twelve pounders,
from which thundering salutes were fired on every
possible occasion. He gave command of this fort
to Captain Beckley, and over it flung his new flag
to the breeze.

He sent his flag to China at the masthead of a
ship he had purchased for the sandalwood trade.
The captain of this ship, Alexander Adams, found
trouble waiting for him at Canton, "because the
Chinese authorities refused to recognise the Hawaiian flag, which had never before been seen in
that port."   We have the statement on good authority that Captain Adams had to pay such heavy
harbour dues that the report thereof to Ka-meha-
meha taught the Hawaiian king one of the principles of civilised business, *i. e.,* to charge fees for
every boat entering his harbour. He lost about
$3,000 in this voyage to China, "chiefly owing to
the new flag."   The lesson learned concerning the
harbour dues was probably worth all that was lost,
although the king lived less than two years afterwards to enjoy his new source of income.

The flag has figured prominently in several international episodes.

The Hawaiian Islands were fertile fields to
greedy land-loving rovers of the seas. In 1842

and 1843 Mr. Charlton, an English consul, made trouble for the Hawaiian chiefs by laying claim to a very valuable piece of land in Honolulu, which the chiefs claimed could not possibly have been given to him by the rightful owners. This was the foundation of a series of disagreements. The consul was an open advocate of English annexation, and reported a dangerous state of affairs to England. Finally, leaving his consulate in the hands of a friend, he went to England to present his own claims. Meanwhile, a captain of an English frigate, Lord George Paulet, was sent to Honolulu. He seized upon every pretext for advancing his intention of seizing the islands in the name of the English crown. The king, Ka-meha-meha III, meanwhile made earnest protest and planned resistance, but his wise counsellors persuaded him not to give Lord Paulet any pretext for action, but to forestall him by making a provisional cession of the kingdom pending the appeal to the protection of the United States and England. On February 25, 1843, the Hawaiian flag was hauled down and the Union Jack was once more raised over a part of the islands. On February 25, 1794, forty-nine years before, Vancouver's flag-raising ceremony had taken place. Like Vancouver, Lord Paulet evidently had little doubt about England's glad welcome of a new colonial possession.

Ka-meha-meha III made a short speech of protest, closing with the words: "I have hope that the life of the land will be restored when my conduct shall be justified." Lord Paulet then took possession of the fort, confiscated Hawaiian ships, compelled natives to enlist to form an English army, and began to increase taxes to meet the expenses of his new government. The king withdrew to another island, and, with his cabinet, disclaimed the authority of Lord Paulet, and continued to appeal to England.

This triumphal flight of the English flag was not at all permanent. In the first part of July, about four months and a half after Lord Paulet's seizure of the islands, Commodore Kearney, in the old U. S. frigate *Constitution,* entered Honolulu harbour. The native chiefs visited his ship. Lord Paulet had collected all the Hawaiian flags and destroyed them, but a new flag was hastily made and raised over the visitors, and a salute fired in its honour—to Lord Paulet's helpless indignation.

However, in the new flag the colors of the bars were permanently reversed. In this respect the modern Hawaiian flag is different from the flag first made.

A few days later Admiral Thomas, commander of the English navy in the Pacific, arrived in Honolulu, and "in most courteous terms solicited a personal interview with the king." In a few hours it became known that he had come to restore the independence of the islands.

On Monday morning, July 31, 1843, the admiral

issued a proclamation restoring the islands to their king, and incidentally mentioning in high terms the work of the American missionaries. Monday forenoon "a parade of several hundred English marines appeared on the plain of Honolulu (now known as Thomas Square), with their officers, their banners waving proudly and their arms glittering in the sunbeams. Admiral Thomas and the suspended king proceeded thither in a carriage, attended by the chiefs and a vast multitude of people. The English standard bearers advanced towards his majesty, their flags bowed gracefully, and a broad, beautiful Hawaiian banner, exhibiting a crown and olive branch, was unfurled over the heads of the king and his attending chieftains. This was saluted by the English troops with field pieces, then by the guns of Lord Paulet's ship, whose yards were manned in homage to the restored sovereign. Then succeeded the roar of the guns of the fort, Punchbowl battery, the admiral's ship, the United States ships and others."

"Thomas Square" was so named and set apart as a perpetual park near the heart of the city, in honour of this action of Admiral Thomas. Monday afternoon the king and chiefs and several thousand people gathered in the new native stone church, Kawaiahao, and held an enthusiastic praise meeting. The king in an eloquent speech uttered a motto worthy of the highest statesmanship. This was later adopted as the national motto and inscribed on all Hawaiian coins: *Ua mau ke ea o ka aina i ka pono*—"Perpetuated is the life of the land by its righteousness," or "The perpetuation of the life of the land depends upon the righteousness thereof." The church was beautifully decorated and on the pulpit was the restored Hawaiian flag. The "army" enlisted by Lord Paulet gladly renounced allegiance to England. The ships were restored and the king's cabinet again took the reins of government. It was not long before word came that Europe and America had, as early as April, recognised the independence of the Hawaiian Kingdom.

Undeterred by this English experience, a Frenchman thought it worth his while to secure the little kingdom. In 1849 Admiral Tromelin sailed into Honolulu harbour and made some emphatic demands, alleging that the king had unlawfully fined a French ship. The king replied that the ship had violated his laws and was necessarily held responsible. The admiral at once landed an armed force with field pieces and scaling ladders and captured the fort. The king, however, had withdrawn his troops, leaving an empty fort with the Hawaiian flag flying from its staff. The Frenchman did not quite dare to pull that flag down in the face of very earnest protests from both the English and American consuls. The French smashed calabashes, spiked the guns, poured powder into the harbour, wrote on the walls of the fort that they were *"Les*

Braves" and then withdrew, turning their trouble over to their home government. For nearly two years the French made trouble. At last the king, Ka-meha-meha III, became tired and placed his kingdom "provisionally under the protection of the United States," declaring that the protectorate should be "perpetual" if the relations with France were not placed on a better footing. The Frenchmen soon discovered that the difficulties could be easily settled, and the long list of grievances "were reduced to two points, *viz.*, the liberty of Catholic worship and the trade in spirits." This last meant the abundant entrance of French brandy. "Nothing more was heard of the rest of the demands."

Flag episodes after these experiences were limited to ordinary affairs of government. Sometimes it floated proudly over fort and palace, while salutes were fired from men-of-war entering the harbour. Sometimes it hung at half mast over the palace while the body of some member of the royal family or some one of high chief blood lay in state. Sometimes its absence from the palace marked the king's departure for some other island. Its reappearance was the signal of the king's return. It floated over ministers' and consuls' offices in different parts of the world and fulfilled its modest duty as the representative of one of "the little kings."

Then came the turbulent times of internal dissension through the reign of Kalakaua and that of his sister, Liliuokalani, resulting in the overthrow of the monarchy in 1893. January 14, 1893, the queen thought herself strong enough to abrogate the Constitution of the islands and promulgate a new Constitution suited to her own wishes. She found that she had opened a volcano under her feet. She prorogued the Legislature in the forenoon and attempted to install her new Constitution. Her cabinet objected. A group of prominent citizens strengthened the cabinet. An impromptu mass meeting was held in the afternoon and a committee of public safety of thirteen was appointed. This was Saturday. Sunday was a day of suppressed excitement. Monday, January 16, over 1,300 citizens gathered in the armory and authorised this committee of public safety to take such steps as might be necessary. That afternoon at 5 o'clock 300 United States marines and sailors were landed. The marines were stationed at the American legation and the sailors at Arion Hall.

The next day, January 17, the committee of public safety issued the following proclamation:

"First—The Hawaiian monarchial system of government is hereby abrogated.

"Second—A Provisional Government for the control and management of public affairs and the protection of public peace is hereby established, to exist until terms of union with the United States of America have been negotiated and agreed upon."

This Provisional Government, with President Dole at its head, under the old Hawaiian flag, was at once recognised, under date of January 17, as the "de facto government of the Hawaiian Islands," by Minister Stevens of the United States. January 18, ministers and consul-generals from several nations hastened to hand in their recognition of the new government, and on the 19th English and Japanese ministers practically completed the list.

This continued until February 1, 1893, when negotiations had progressed so far that United States Minister Stevens felt safe in raising the Stars and Stripes over the government buildings and declaring a protectorate. This was the fourth time that a far-away representative of a foreign power had felt certain that his annexation of Hawaii would be joyfully received by his home government. And this fourth act was subject to reversal. Five prominent men went to Washington, empowered to make a treaty of annexation with the United States. March 4, 1893, President Cleveland was inaugurated. He withdrew the treaty from consideration by the Senate. Then came the visit of "Paramount Blount," who arrived in Honolulu March 29.

The Provisional Government was strongly entrenched, and Mr. Blount found that the only thing he could do was to withdraw United States protection.

April 1st the announcement was made in the morning papers that the United States flag would be lowered at 11 o'clock, and the Hawaiian flag restored as the emblem of the Provisional Government. For the brief space of almost two months the Stars and Stripes had floated over Hawaii.

Hundreds of people flocked to the spacious grounds around the government buildings. It was a curious crowd—Orientals, Europeans, Africans and Americans—mingling together. The Stars and Stripes slipped down the rattling lines from the flagstaff when the bugle call was sounded. "There was another gleam of colour and the Hawaiian flag crawled up the now taut ropes and shook itself free, its blue, white and crimson bars floating in their accustomed place. The silence was undisturbed. The troops of the Provisional Government presented arms, but the American men-of-war in the harbour did not salute the restored flag."

As time passed, President Cleveland's desire to restore the monarchy became more and more apparent, and under the same old Hawaiian colours, "on July 4, 1894, the Constitution of the Republic of Hawaii was promulgated," and all designs for United States interference were thwarted. The beautiful and loved flag of Hawaii, the royal flag from the times of Ka-meha-meha I, the ensign of the Provisional Government, unchanged, became the banner of the first Republic of the Pacific Ocean.

It remained the flag of the Republic until the

news reached Honolulu that President McKinley, on July 7, 1898, had signed the joint resolution of annexation adopted by both houses of Congress.

It was necessary that the officials of the newly annexed islands should take the oath of allegiance to the United States, and that the final change of government should be marked by a new and authorised flag-raising ceremony. Great preparations were made for the solemn exercises attending the transfer of the Republic of Hawaii to the Republic of the United States. On August 12, 1898, thousands of people again crowded into the government grounds. The National Guard of Hawaii and companies of United States marines were drawn up around the former palace. In front of the palace, now the Capitol Building, was a grandstand, about which the Hawaiian and United States colours were intertwined.

The Hawaiian and United States officials, the diplomatic corps and a few friends filled the grandstand. After prayers came the formal transfer of sovereignty.

The final salute to the Hawaiian emblem of an independent nation was fired. As the last report died away in echoes among the surrounding hills, the Hawaiian national anthem, "Hawaii Ponoi," in solemn grandeur, stirred the hearts of the multitude. Mrs. Garland, an eye-witness, said: "The music ceased and for one instant the Hawaiian flag still floated, then as it was slowly lowered, utter stillness held every one mute. A great wave of intense feeling seemed to flow over the people. For the moment we were in a country without a flag. There were few who did not weep. Then a clear sounding call from the bugles of the s. s., *Philadelphia,* a sudden stir through all the throng, and then with the triumphant ringing strains of the 'Star Spangled Banner,' up rose majestically our own dear flag, reaching the truck with the last grand chord. Three mighty cheers burst forth. Men grasped each other by the hand, and hats and handkerchiefs waved. A group of Hawaiian young women stood behind us. As the Stars and Stripes went up, from one came the repressed exclamation, 'Oh, you beautiful thing.' "

Then President Dole and his cabinet took the oath of allegiance to the United States. The soldiers marched to their barracks to be sworn into their new service. The crowd dispersed, while salutes were fired from the ships in the harbour. The American flag floats in its own influential place over the palace, not as a kingly, but as a republican flag. The Hawaiian flag still floats over many a home in the islands, as well as over the corner posts of the old palace under the American flag, as the permanent flag of the Territory of Hawaii.

The Hawaiian flag is surrounded by many historical memories which mean much to residents of both native and foreign descent, and they rejoice that the dear old flag is not lost from the nation's history. As one writer says, this feeling shows that "the flag does not represent so much a particular form of government as it does the great heart of the people which throbs beneath."

INDEX

Alexander, W. D., 95, 132, 175.
American Occupation, 211.
Annexation to United States, 213.
Anson, Lord, 99.
Ao-tea-roa, New Zealand, 23.
Aukele-nui-a-iku, 24, 33.

Battle of Sand-hills, 136.
Battle of the Tabu, 181.
Bingham, 184, 188.
Blount, "Paramount," 211.

Campbell, Alexander, 183.
Cession to Great Britain, 201.
Charlton, English Consul, 205.
Condition of people, 194-199.
Constitution, first, 1840, 191-194.
Constitution, Republic, 212.
Constitution, United States frigate, 206.
Cook, Captain, as god Lono, 101-112.
Cook, Captain, four accounts, 101.
Cook, Captain, death, 112.

Davis, Isaac, 155, 160, 193.
Declaration of Rights, 193.
Decrease of population, 161.
Dole, Sanford B., 210.
Dragon, 24-33.

Ellis, William, 43, 187.

First Bible printing, 187.
First hymn-book, 186.
First printing, 184, 185.
Flag, Hawaiian, 200-215.
Flag, colors reversed, 206.
Flag, Territorial, 214.
Fornander, 79, 95, 99, 143, 151, 155.
French, occupation, 208.

Gaetano, 1555, 96, 99.
Grey, Sir George, 14.

Hawaii, Owhyhee, 41, 107.
Hawaii, Polynesia, 42.
Hawaii from Java, Sata, 38.
Hawaii-loa-Viking, 36-40.
Hawa-iki, 22, 42, 45.
Hewa-hewa, high priest, 180.
Hine-nui-a-te-po, 20, 24.

Ivory, whales' teeth, 116.

Ka-ahu - manu - breaking tabu, 177, 180.
Ka-hekili, 114, 133, 144, 149, 159.
Ka-ha-hana, 114, 123, 144.
Kai-ana, 155.
Ka-la-kaua, 209.
Ka-lani-opun, 106, 111, 125, 140, 165.
Kalola-Ka-hekili's sister, 111, 140.

217

Ka-meha-meha, 65, 78, 127, 155, 162, 179, 201.

Ka-meha-meha II, 179, 180, 185.

Ka-meha-meha III, 180, 190, 205, 207.

Ka-pa-wa, 73, 76.

Ka-o-pulu-pulu, 119, 147.

Kearney, Commodore, 1843, 206.

Ke-ku-hau-pio, 126.

Ki-wa-la-o, 141, 165.

Ku-alii, 98.

Kua-i-Helani, 24.

Kua-kini, Gov. Adams, 183, 185.

Ku-kana-loa, first white man, 94.

Ku-lou, kneeling, 94.

Ku-waha-ilo, Pale's father, 28.

Laa from Tahiti, 86-91.

Liliu-o-ka-lani, 209.

Magna Charta, 192.

Maui legends, 14-23.

Max Muller, Av-iki, 45.

Menehunes, workmen, 39.

Moi-keha, 79, 86.

Nana-ulu, 53, 73.

Paao from Samoa, 65, 78, 133.

Pau-makua, 95, 143.

Port regulations, 186.

Provisional Government, 210, 213.

Republic of Hawaii, 212.

Restoration of flag, 207.

Saavedra, 1527, 94.

Smith, Hon. S. Percy, 45.

Stars, 37.

Taxes, 195.

Thomas, Admiral, 206.

Thomas Square, 207.

Tregear, Edward, 45.

Ulu, King of Hawaii, 47, 73.

Ulu-Ur of the Chaldeas, 36.

Vancouver, Cession of Hawaii, 200, 205.

Vikings of the Pacific, 36, 40, 95.

Young, John, 155, 160.